Messiah, the World's Only Hope

Messiah, the World's Only Hope

Christ in Isaiah

This inductive Bible study is designed for individual, small group, or classroom use. A leader's guide with full lesson plans and the answers to the Bible study questions is available from Regular Baptist Press. Order RBP1735 online at www.regularbaptistpress.org, e-mail orders@rbpstore.org, call toll-free 1-800-727-4440, or contact your distributor.

REGULAR BAPTIST PRESS
1300 North Meacham Road
Schaumburg, Illinois 60173-4806

The Doctrinal Basis of Our Curriculum

A more detailed statement with references is available upon request.

- The verbal, plenary inspiration of the Scriptures
- Only one true God
- The Trinity of the Godhead
- The Holy Spirit and His ministry
- The personality of Satan
- The Genesis account of creation
- Original sin and the fall of man
- The virgin birth of Christ
- Salvation through faith in the shed blood of Christ
- The bodily resurrection and priesthood of Christ
- Grace and the new birth
- Justification by faith
- Sanctification of the believer
- The security of the believer
- The church
- The ordinances of the local church: baptism by immersion and the Lord's Supper
- Biblical separation—ecclesiastical and personal
- Obedience to civil government
- The place of Israel
- The pretribulation rapture of the church
- The premillennial return of Christ
- The millennial reign of Christ
- Eternal glory in Heaven for the righteous
- Eternal torment in Hell for the wicked

MESSIAH, THE WORLD'S ONLY HOPE: CHRIST IN ISAIAH
Adult Bible Study Book
Vol. 57, No. 2

Regular Baptist Press • Schaumburg, Illinois
www.regularbaptistpress.org • 1-800-727-4440
Printed in U.S.A.

RBP1738 • ISBN: 978-1-59402-674-4

Contents

Preface

On what are you pinning your hopes? Everyone needs hope in something or someone. Too many uncertainties fill our lives for us to continue without hope. Some people put hope in themselves. They work hard to control every aspect of their lives. Others put their hope in money and things, thinking that they will have enough resources to buy their way out of uncertainties. Still others put their hope in people, like a spouse or a friend, to give them stability and to rescue them when their lives fall apart.

But the hope for the world is not hard work, money, or people. The world will find true hope in only one Person, Jesus Christ. Messiah, the World's Only Hope presents Christ from the pen of the prophet Isaiah. Isaiah wrote his book of prophecy at a dark time in the history of Judah, a time when the nation was running out of hope. His prophecies on Christ gave hope to Judah. As you study Christ in Isaiah, you also will find confidence for now and hope for the future.

As you study this course, depend on the Lord to help you understand the solid hope available in Christ. If you are doubting that Christ is the answer to your struggles, if you are wavering in your faith, or if you don't know much about Christ, then the message of hope will be particularly encouraging to you.

Lesson 1

Needed: A Messiah

God's grace is greater than sin.

Isaiah 1

"Come now, and let us reason together, saith the LORD: though your sins be as scarlet, they shall be a white as snow; though they be red like crimson, they shall be as wool" (Isaiah 1:18).

Our lives are filled with fakes. We have fake leather, fake plants, fake jewelry, fake furs, fake suntans, fake hair, fake food, and even fake teeth. In fact, it is quite plausible to say that no one can get through a day without using something fake. For the most part, we don't care if something is not real. Without thinking twice, we guzzle down "orange juice" for breakfast that actually is mostly water and a smorgasbord of chemicals.

While we are okay eating fake food with our fake teeth, we are usually not okay with insincere people. We want our relationships to be real. God is no different. He wants us to be real with Him, too.

Getting Started

1. Approximately how many different fake items do you own?

2. Why do most people want their relationships to be real?

Searching the Scriptures

At the time of Isaiah, Judah was in need of getting real. Their lives were fake and God challenged them about it. God's challenge also translates to our need to be real with God.

The Northern Kingdom of Israel fell (722 BC) to the Assyrians during the reign of Ahaz, the third king mentioned in Isaiah 1:1. The Southern Kingdom of Judah fell to the Babylonians about a century after Isaiah's time. (The final destruction of Jerusalem occurred in 586 BC.) Isaiah witnessed Israel's fall as well as the Lord's threats against Judah. Isaiah warned Judah of her need to turn to God to avoid a fate similar to Israel's. He predicted that Judah would be taken captive by Babylon; but he also prophesied of Judah's return from captivity and of the ultimate deliverance God would bring through the Messiah's ministry. Today's study reveals Judah's need for a Messiah and anticipates God's provision of one.

You could call the opening chapter of Isaiah "The Great Arraignment." God set forth His grievances against Judah, illustrated the evidences, exhorted the people to change their ways, and challenged them to a trial.

Ignorance of Their Relationship to God

God was the speaker in this chapter. He called upon Heaven and earth as witnesses of the relationship between His people and Him: "Hear, O heavens, and give ear, O earth: for the Lord hath spoken" (v. 2). Israel's ignorance shown in her rebellion, stupidity, and sin.

3. Read Isaiah 1:2. What do we learn about the people of Judah by God's comparison of them to rebellious children?

Isaiah compared Israel to a rebellious child who, despite his good upbringing, ignorantly rebels against his parents, who gave him life.

Most people consider the ox a stupid animal, and they know that the donkey is stubborn, but both the ox and the donkey manifest more sense than Israel did. Even an animal knows its owner, who feeds it (v. 3). But Israel was ignorant of the God Who created and sustained her.

Note the words of verse 4, which depict the people's sin. The people of Israel spurned God and turned from Him, showing their ignorance. How different from what God intended for His people!

Indifference to Chastisement

God had disciplined Israel's sin, but the nation was indifferent to it. He asked, "Why should ye be stricken any more?" (v. 5). Their continuing rebellion brought repeated punishment; however, it was without effect.

Isaiah compared the nation to a bruised and bloody body. Outside (the head) and inside (the heart), from bottom (the sole of the foot) to top (the head), the body was afflicted. The various words Isaiah used to describe the body's injuries reflect different sources for the hurt. "Wounds" are from a sword; "bruises" the result of a blow; "putrefying sores" from a whipping. Although God had tried to get Israel's attention through discipline, she did not respond and made no attempt to correct her problems. The nation remained indifferent to God's chastening hand.

4. What might be some reasons a person would ignore God's chastening hand?

The Assyrians did not conquer Judah, but they did attack, even threatening the city of Jerusalem (see Isaiah 36 and 37). Only the hand of God kept the whole nation from being conquered.

Insincerity in Their Worship

The Jews of Isaiah's day probably felt they didn't deserve God's punishment. After all, they were still quite religious. Even though they still held to God's prescribed sacrificial system, they had abandoned

Him in their hearts. In verses 10–15, God addressed the matter of Judah's worship.

5. Read Isaiah 1:10–15. What three words would you use to describe Judah's worship of God?

The people offered unacceptable sacrifices. Why were they unacceptable? In short, it was because Judah's worship had become a matter of form; their relationship had decayed into superficial religion. They were guilty going through the motions with no sincerity of heart in their worship. The people had shown as little respect for God as an animal who tramples something underfoot (v. 12). Their worship was an "abomination" (v. 13), a word usually used of pagan worship.

Judah even observed the appointed holy days, but God had tired of the people's observances since they did not observe those days with a sincere heart. God rejected their empty formality so much, that He would not even hear their prayers. They were as guilty as murderers were; their hands were "full of blood" (v. 15).

6. What questions could you ask yourself as you examined your sinfulness and sincerity before God?

Change Your Path

Having demonstrated that His people were sinful, both in act and in attitude, God presented them with a challenge. He wanted them to stop their wicked ways (v. 16).

7. Read Isaiah 1:16. Why are the words "before mine eyes" so important in God's instructions to Judah?

Judah needed to do more than just stop sinning; they also needed to begin doing good (v. 17).

8. Read Isaiah 1:17. In His instructions to Judah, why would God mention doing good to rather insignificant orphans and widows?

Orphans and widows were a downtrodden class of people, usually destitute and preyed upon by the unscrupulous and without anyone to champion their cause. God would see justice for them.

Consider His Pardon

Isaiah 1:18 is actually a challenge to go to trial. In view of the case that God had against His people, there was little hope for them. Their sins were as brilliantly red as scarlet, as bright as crimson, and God had to judge them as such. Only when the offender acknowledges his guilt can the offended pardon him or her. Hence, God proposed a trial in which He could find Israel only guilty. Then He would offer pardon and cleansing. Their blood-colored sins could become as white as snow.

How can God offer pardon to sinful man? We find the answers to these questions in the redemptive work of Christ. At this point in Israel's history, Messiah had not yet come. The pardon God offered was based on the belief that the Messiah would come. Later in the book, Isaiah prophesied of the coming Messiah and His pardon.

An individual's response to the challenge of verse 18 determined whether he or she would experience blessing or judgment; it was either eat or be eaten. Respond and eat (v. 19): The obedient would enjoy the bountiful harvest God had promised in Deuteronomy 28:3–6. Or, refuse and be eaten (v. 20): The disobedient rebels would be eaten ("devoured") by the enemy ("sword") as promised in Deuteronomy 28:45–52. The seriousness of these promises and warnings is underscored by the words "for the mouth of the Lord hath spoken it" (v. 20).

9. Based on God's warnings and promises in Isaiah 1:18–20, what would you expect Judah's response to be?

Ultimately, Judah doesn't repent and do good works. Looking back at their choices, it is easy to be critical of them. However, we as believers today can be just as stubborn and ignorant of our sin.

In the final section of chapter 1, God continued to point out the sins of His people and warned that judgment would come. This judgment had the goal of getting His people to turn from their sins.

Corruption

The decline of the nation was evident. In the past, Jerusalem had been faithful to God, but in Isaiah's day, she had broken her covenant vows like a harlot (v. 21).

Silver and wine were valuable commodities in the ancient Middle East. But the Israelites were no longer valuable; instead they were as worthless as the residue left after silver had been smelted ("dross") or as worthless as diluted, watered-down wine.

The corrupt leaders who ignored the plight of orphans and widows were also evidence of the nation's decline (v. 23). Furthermore, bribery was rampant; justice was only for those who could afford to pay the bribe.

Correction

In verse 24 God promised that sin would not continue indefinitely. Judgment was sure to occur, and He would rid Himself ("ease me") of the wicked, even if those people were supposedly His followers.

God didn't intend His chastisement to be vindictive but rather to accomplish a purpose.

10. Isaiah 1:25. Why is purging dross a good analogy for what God wanted to do to Judah?

In the Millennium, Jerusalem will once again be a faithful city. During that time, God will reinstitute the ancient system of judges to rule the kingdom, as He did before the kings.

Conversion

The purpose of chastisement is to bring man to repentance. Unfortunately, not all people respond the way God would want. Some repent (v. 27), but others rebel (v. 28).

God will purge rebels from the kingdom, leaving only the faithful remnant. Sadly, the majority of Judah rejected the pardon God provided. The final verses of Isaiah 1 describe the fate.

11. Read Isaiah 1:29–31. Theses verses give a bleak outlook for those in Judah who refused to repent. How do you see God's grace even in these bleak verses?

Making It Personal

12. Write a statement of praise about God's grace.

13. Review the self-examination questions you listed under question 6. Take time this week to make sure you are living a genuine life before God.

14. Memorize Isaiah 1:18.

Lesson 2

The Messenger for the Messiah

God is looking for people who will serve Him faithfully.

Isaiah 6

"Also I heard the voice of the Lord, saying, Whom shall I send, and who will go for us? Then said I, Here am I; send me" (Isaiah 6:8).

In the past, looking for a job required searching the newspaper or knocking on the door of a business. Now there is less shoe leather and ink involved when someone wants a job. While newspapers and walk-in inquires still work, a lot of job searching today is done on the Internet. In fact, people can now post their résumés on several different Web sites and let businesses come looking for them. Of course, this means that a professional looking résumé is important if a person wants to attract employers.

This study is about Isaiah's job interview as conducted by God. Isaiah didn't need a résumé, though, for God already knew everything about him.

Getting Started

1. How would you go about finding a job?

2. How dependent would you be on Internet sites such as Jobfox or Headhunters?

3. How does God go about finding personnel to serve Him?

Searching the Scriptures

God's call of Isaiah to ministry set the stage for some of the most outstanding prophecies concerning the Messiah. Isaiah truly was a messenger of the Messiah.

Confrontation with God

"In the year that king Uzziah died I saw also the Lord sitting upon a throne, high and lifted up, and his train filled the temple" (Isaiah 6:1). Isaiah's vision of God eclipsed the splendor of any Judean king. God's throne is exalted above any earthly throne.

Verse 2 tells us that part of this revelation of God included servants of God, the seraphim: "Above it stood the seraphims: each one had six wings; with twain he covered his face, and with twain he covered his feet, and with twain he did fly."

Seraphim are an order of celestial beings. Each seraph has three pairs of wings. The seraph uses one pair of wings to cover his face. This is most likely a symbol of humility. The second set of wings covers his feet in order to show respect. The Seraph uses the last set of wings for flying, suggesting service. God has an innumerable number of angelic beings who serve Him. The attitude these beings displayed should challenge believers today.

The antiphonal worship of verse 3 emphasizes God's holiness. The threefold repetition of the word "holy" was for emphasis, a common literary device used in the Bible. The One Whom Isaiah saw in His splendor was perfectly holy.

4. Are God's holiness and majesty duly recognized in Christian worship today? How? Why?

5. How can the believer show greater respect for the majesty and holiness of God?

Too many people tend to think of God as a buddy or a doting grandfather. They don't respect His majesty and holiness. The relationship between this attitude toward God and the decline of moral values today is obvious.

"And the posts of the door moved at the voice of him that cried, and the house was filled with smoke" (v. 4). The "voice" belonged to one of the seraphim declaring God's holiness. The smoke here is probably the same as the cloud that led the Israelites through the wilderness. The shaking of the doorposts and the smoke were evidences of God's power and presence.

6. How does a long gaze at God help to prepare a person for serving God?

Confession of Sin

7. Read Matthew 17:1–8, Acts 9:1–7, and Revelation 1:9–17. How did the person who had an encounter with God or Christ in each passage react?

8. What is a common element in the three responses?

Isaiah responded to his encounter with God much like the others who had similar experiences. He recognized himself for what he was. One cannot see God in His majesty and holiness without seeing the utter sinfulness of self.

"Then said I, Woe is me! for I am undone; because I am a man of unclean lips, and I dwell in the midst of a people of unclean lips." The Bible does not record any personal sin of Isaiah. To be sure, he was a sinner as are all men (Romans 3:23), but from the facts given about his life, we may conclude that Isaiah was a godly man. Nevertheless, when he saw the Lord, the experience forced him to confront and confess his own sinfulness. He pronounced a woe on himself, for he realized that he, too, was subject to judgment.

9. Why is examining your heart in the light of God's glory crucial to preparing to serve God?

"For mine eyes have seen the King, the Lord of hosts" (Isaiah 6:5). Because Isaiah had seen God, he responded with "Woe is me." He recognized that the King of Kings was far superior to King Uzziah. Before *the* King, the "Lord of hosts" (armies), he submitted himself with humility.

Cleansing from Sin

One of the seraphim took a coal from one of the temple's two altars: the brazen altar (in the frontcourt of the temple), which had a continual fire, and the altar of incense (before the Holy of Holies), which had a fire in the morning and the evening (v. 6). "And he laid it upon my mouth, and said, Lo, this hath touched thy lips; and thine iniquity is taken away, and thy sin purged" (v. 7). This action is symbolic of the removal of Isaiah's sin. Note that cleansing cannot come until a person acknowledges his or her guilt. Not only Isaiah but also his whole nation needed cleansing.

10. What goes through your mind when you think of an angel applying a hot coal to Isaiah's lips?

11. How does the account help you to see the seriousness of sin in the life of a potential servant of God?

Calling by God

It wasn't until Isaiah had encountered God, confessed his sinfulness, and been cleansed that God expressed His need of a messenger. The call of God follows the cleansing by God.

12. Could it be that many Christians do not know God's will for their lives because they have not experienced His daily cleansing? Explain.

"Also I heard the voice of the Lord, saying, Whom shall I send?" (v. 8). God is still looking for people who will serve Him. Although heavenly beings devoted to His service surround Him, He chooses human beings to bear the message of the good news of salvation.

13. Why is the belief that God couldn't use you to do much for Him a sinful attitude?

Commitment to Service

Isaiah was ready to respond. "Then said I, Here am I; send me" (v.

8). Isaiah responded to the Lord just as the disciples (Matthew 4:18–22; 9:9). Each was willing to obey his King (Isaiah 6:5; Matthew 27:37). Because a king commands absolute obedience, the believer should always respond immediately to God.

14. Isaiah committed to do a job for God even though he knew nothing about it. What does that say about his faith and trust in God?

To some, Isaiah's response might seem to be an irrational act. After all, Isaiah didn't really have much information about the job. Shouldn't he have asked about the job description and what God expected of him? And what about the pay or the hours? What were the opportunities for advancement, or what were the perks? Neither Isaiah nor the Lord addressed such matters. Isaiah accepted the challenge, not knowing what was involved. This is how we are to respond to the King of Kings.

Commission to Service

When God first called Isaiah, the prophet may have thought that his nation would also seek cleansing just as he had. Unfortunately, this was not the case.

God accepted Isaiah's offer of himself, telling him to "go" (v. 9). Isaiah was to proclaim a negative message, and the response to Isaiah's ministry wouldn't be positive (v. 10).

15. How would you like God to call you to a ministry that would never bear any fruit?

Most preachers prefer to proclaim a positive message. However, the Bible also contains negative messages of discipline and judgment. The disobedience of God's people made discipline necessary. In spite of Isaiah's faithful preaching, the nation as a whole would not hear the message.

"Then said I, Lord, how long?" (v. 11). For the first time, Isaiah inquired about the job he had accepted so quickly. Maybe he hoped the job would be brief, that he'd soon be able to preach a message the people would accept.

In the American military, enlisted personnel sign up for a specified duration, and they can choose the area of service in which they want training. The military will commission recruits for a given number of years. God, however, gave Isaiah an open-ended contract. He did not get a job choice or a limited period of service.

As long as there were people around him, Isaiah was to minister (vv. 11, 12). The wasted cities, uninhabited houses, and desolate land refer to the captivity that Isaiah and other prophets were predicting. This captivity did not occur in Isaiah's day; it was not until a century later that the Babylonians conquered Jerusalem and carried off the captive Jews.

16. What do you think motivated Isaiah to get out of bed every morning?

17. What can we learn from Isaiah's motivation for ministry?

Promised Remnant

Isaiah could have become discouraged because of the poor response to his message, but a faithful group remained. There will always be a remnant that remains faithful. God compared the remnant to felled trees that still have life in the roots and stumps (v. 13). Although Babylon took most of Judah into captivity, a few of the people remained in the land. Others returned after the fall of Babylon, and from this group a faithful remnant continued.

Believers today are a part of God's remnant. Like Isaiah of old, we live among unbelieving people. Yet we must remain faithful to God even in the middle of distressing circumstances and rejection by the majority of those around us. God has set us as lights in a dark place to bear testimony to His saving power.

Making It Personal

18. How can you take a long look at God?

19. The better you know God the more you will see the sin in your life. Confess your sin and keep your heart pure so that you are ready to serve the Lord.

20. Memorize Isaiah 6:8.

Lesson 3

The Virgin-born Messiah

Israel's prophesied that the Messiah would be born of a virgin.

Isaiah 7:1–25

"Therefore the Lord himself shall give you a sign; Behold, a virgin shall conceive, and bear a son, and shall call his Immanuel" (Isaiah 7:14).

On June 30, 1970, a mother in Omaha, Nebraska, gave birth to twin boys. The boys weighed in at nine pounds, six ounces and eight pounds, fourteen ounces. The twins set a record for the state of Nebraska at that time. When the boys tell people what they weighed at birth, the response is always, "Your poor mother!"

That was a "big" birth, but no birth is as big as the birth of Christ. He was born of a virgin, not as a display of God's power, but of necessity. This Bible study examines the importance of the Virgin Birth of Christ.

Getting Started

1. What, if anything was unusual about your birth?

2. What unusual births have you heard of or perhaps been a part of?

Searching the Scriptures

The prophesy of the Virgin Birth appears in Isaiah 7:14. The context to the prophecy helps the reader to understand better the background of the announcement. The date of this account was about 734 BC, roughly twelve years before the fall of the Northern Kingdom of Israel. Assyria was the leading world power of the day and a serious threat to all the nations around it.

The Peril

For Judah to face political peril was not a new situation. The Assyrian Empire was expanding, and no nation had been able to turn it back. Assyria was known for their cruelty toward their enemies.

The leaders of the two threatened nations, Syria and Israel, reacted against the Assyrians by forming an alliance. Rezin, king of Syria, and Pekah, king of Israel, wanted Judah to join their coalition to form a stronger resistance. However, Ahaz, the king of Judah, had already decided to align himself with the Assyrians. Not wishing to have an enemy on both sides of them, Rezin and Pekah attacked Judah (Isaiah 7:1) in order to depose Ahaz and install a puppet king who would join their confederacy (v. 6). These two kings did much damage to Judah (2 Chronicles 28).

3. Read 2 Chronicles 28:5–8. What damage did Israel and Syria cause Judah?

4. Why did they cause damage to Judah (v. 6)?

Although Jerusalem did not fall to the Israeli-Syrian confederacy, the coalition caused both the king of Judah and his people much concern. Isaiah wrote that the hearts of the people were moved like tree branches in the wind (v. 2). They faced some tough questions: Would Jerusalem fall prey to the confederacy's attack? Would the country experience further destruction?

The Promise

God never gives promises without purpose or background, and His promises always suggest an improvement of circumstances. The grave situation facing the king of Judah provided an excellent background for a promise from God.

5. What promises might Ahaz and Judah have been interested in at this point in Judah's history?

The Lord told Isaiah to meet the king at a reservoir. The king was probably inspecting the water supply in view of an imminent siege of the city. A supply of water was critical during a siege. Isaiah was to take his son Shearjashub ("a remnant shall return") along.

Isaiah's message was a consolation to the fearful king: Watch out, calm down, and don't be afraid. Don't be discouraged because of the plotting of the two enemies (v. 4). Like smoldering sticks, their fire would soon go out.

In Isaiah 7:5 and 6, Isaiah told the plans of the conspirators to Ahaz. Rezin and Pekah wanted to divide Judah between them and install a puppet king in the place of Ahaz.

6. Read 2 Kings 16. What did Ahaz do as king?

7. What did Ahaz deserve in the way of protection from God?

8. What did Ahaz deserve in the way of promises from God?

The Word of the Lord

Isaiah first announced that the conspiracy would not accomplish its goal (v. 7); then he predicted that within sixty-five years both Damascus—the capital city of Syria, where Rezin ruled—and Samaria—the capital city of Israel (called Ephraim in v. 9), where Pekah reigned—would be destroyed. As it turned out, both Rezin and Pekah died within two years of this prophecy. Furthermore, Damascus fell to the Assyrians in 732 BC (two years after this prophecy), and Israel fell in 722 BC (twelve years after the prophecy). Israel was taken into captivity, and then the Assyrians filled the land of Israel with foreign colonists so that by 669 BC ("within sixty-five years"), Israel was so shattered and fragmented that it was impossible for her to unite as a nation.

Isaiah's word closed with a warning to Ahaz. He told him that if he did not believe, then he would not be established (v. 9). Isaiah's message was not only to the king but to the king's people as well. Judah had trusted Assyria rather than the Lord so that even with the removal of the two threatening enemies, her plight was worse. The Assyrians overran her and subjected her.

The Sign

Obviously, Ahaz did not believe God's message given through Isaiah. Yet God graciously offered to show Ahaz a sign—any sign—to authenticate Isaiah's message (v. 10). It is obvious that God wanted to give a sign. It is also obvious that Ahaz would not have asked for the particular sign that God eventually gave.

But Ahaz rejected the sign. His response, "I will not ask, neither will I tempt the Lord," did not indicate his piety but rather his unbelief (v. 12). God had told him to ask for a sign; He didn't merely offer a sign if Ahaz felt he needed one. Isaiah saw that Ahaz was trying God's patience: "But will ye weary my God also?" he asked (v. 13).

The promised sign of Isaiah 7:14 is one of the grandest prophecies of the Bible. It is a cardinal doctrine and a fundamental of our faith. Denying the truth is to be unchristian. Yet liberal theologians have attacked this precious truth and unbelievers have scorned it.

"Therefore the Lord himself shall give you a sign; Behold, a virgin shall conceive, and bear a son, and shall call his name Immanuel" (v. 14). The Lord gave this sign, not just to Ahaz but to the "house of David" (v. 13). Therefore, the prophecy continues.

9. Read Isaiah 7:14 and Matthew 1:22 and 23. How sure is Matthew that Isaiah 7:14 is fulfilled in Christ?

While Matthew 1:23 confirms that the passage is a prophecy concerning Christ, there remains the problem of how to interpret Isaiah 7:15 and 16.

10. Read Isaiah 7:15 and 16. What problems do you see in interpreting Isaiah 7:15 and 16?

While Isaiah 7:15 and 16 is difficult to rectify with the historical setting in which Isaiah gave it, it undoubtedly relates to the birth of Christ. Matthew's use of the passage makes the connection clear.

11. How should the promise of Immanuel, meaning God with us, have affected Ahaz?

12. What would it have meant to those who witnessed the birth of Christ?

13. What does the fulfilled promise mean to you today?

The Significance

The teaching of the Virgin Birth is of such importance that it merits a discussion.

14. Why is the Virgin Birth important?

The entire doctrine of Christ and the trustworthiness of the gospel are dependent on the Virgin Birth. To doubt it is to undermine Christianity and bring about several damaging consequences to the message of the Bible. First, God could not give a revelation of Himself in bodily form without the Virgin Birth. Second, denying the Virgin Birth discredits Christ's purpose for coming into the world—to bring salvation to hopeless humanity. Third, Jesus' present intercessory ministry could not exist if He was not virgin born. Last, denying the Virgin Birth sets Christ aside from His role as the judge of all the earth.

While it is impossible to discuss at length these propositions, it is nevertheless clear that this doctrine is of fundamental importance.

The Prediction

In Isaiah 7:17, the prophet predicted that the Assyrians would cause a grave crisis in Judah. So wouldn't it have been to Judah's benefit to join Syria and Israel in an effort to resist Assyria? No. Isaiah had just prophesied that the two kings would soon pass from the scene and hence could not help Judah.

Furthermore—and here is the crucial issue—for Judah to have

joined the two neighboring nations to fight the Assyrians would have meant trusting the might of man rather than God. While Ahaz had not joined this confederacy, neither had he trusted God. He worked out an agreement with the Assyrians, but it left him paying tribute to them (2 Kings 16:7, 8). From that day until the fall of the Assyrian kingdom, Judah was a deprived and humiliated nation. Although the Assyrians never conquered Jerusalem, they did devastate the land around it.

The closing verses of chapter seven picture a land that would be overrun by the enemy. Soldiers from Egypt and Assyria ("flies" and "bees") would swarm throughout Judah. God would use the Assyrians ("a hired razor") to humiliate Judah. The land would not be tilled, and plantings of trees and vines would be destroyed. Furthermore, the only food available would be the butter ("curds") from a few cattle grazing the ruined farmland and honey from bees feeding on the wildflowers. This destruction resulted from the people's turning away from God.

Making It Personal

15. King Ahaz's failure to ask for and accept the promise of God had disastrous repercussions upon both himself and his people. What are some promises of God that we tend to ignore today?

16. Choose to trust a promise of God today that you have ignored.

17. Memorize Isaiah 7:14.

Lesson 4

The Beginning of the Mighty King Messiah

The humility Christ displayed at His first coming will be followed by His exaltation.

Isaiah 9:1–7

"For unto us a child is born, unto us a son is given: and the government shall be upon his shoulder: and his name shall be called Wonderful, Counsellor, The mighty God, The everlasting Father, The Prince of Peace" (Isaiah 9:6).

How seriously do you take a little boy who runs around with his toy ax and plastic raincoat telling you that he wants to be a firefighter when he grows up? Some kids actually realize their dreams and become firefighters, but the vast majority don't. Usually we smile and politely acknowledge the child's ambitious statements, realizing he probably will never become a firefighter.

Jesus was different from the typical boy or girl. Jesus knew exactly what He was going to do when He grew up. Prophets predicted what would characterize His ministry. They knew that Jesus would be a humble person.

Getting Started

1. As a kid, what did you want to be when you grew up?

2. What did your parents think you would be?

3. Were either of you right?

Searching the Scriptures

The Old Testament is filled with prophecies concerning various aspects of Christ's life and ministry. The New Testament records the fulfillment of many of them. Some have yet to be fulfilled, but the accurate and literal way the other prophecies have been fulfilled assures us that they will all come to pass just as accurately and literally.

The Need for the Messiah

In the closing verses of Isaiah 8, the prophet predicted a time when God's people would suffer great distress because of sin. The last two verses are referring to the Assyrian invasion in 701 BC.

4. Isaiah 8:11–22. What descriptions of Israel strike you as particularly gloomy?

In Isaiah 9:1, the prophet predicted a change: the gloom of the vexed would pass, and humbling affliction would give way to future honor as Jesus, Israel's Messiah, would come to the region.

Matthew's record of the public ministry of Jesus begins in Galilee. Jesus had been ministering in Judea, but after John's imprisonment, He left Judea and traveled through Samaria to His hometown of Nazareth. After the people there rejected Him (Luke 4:16–30), He left Nazareth and went to Capernaum, and from there He taught and ministered throughout Galilee.

Why did Jesus do this? Matthew explained why: "That it might be fulfilled which was spoken by Esaias the prophet, saying, The land of

Zabulon, and the land of Nephthalim, by the way of the sea, beyond Jordan, Galilee of the Gentiles" (Matthew 4:14, 15). In other words, Jesus' travels fulfilled the prophecy recorded in Isaiah 9:1.

After predicting a change for the people of Judah after Messiah's presence in their region, Isaiah explained that the people saw the light of Christ (v. 2). Matthew also quoted this passage (Matthew 4:16). The Messiah came to give light in a place of darkness; He is the light of the world (John 8:12).

5. Read Ephesians 2:1–10. What is the condition of an unsaved person?

6. How is he made alive, or saved?

7. What is in store for the saved (v. 6)?

People can't give physical life to the dead or spiritual life to the unregenerate. Messiah has the power to do both because He is God. His deity is suggested in the Old Testament and clearly taught in the New Testament. Isaiah 9:6 reads, "For unto us a child is born, unto us a son is given." Some expositors believe the pairing of the two similar phrases is merely a Hebrew poetic device. Others think that the phrase "a child is born" refers to the Messiah's human nature and that "a son is given" refers to His divine nature.

Messiah's Humanity

Jesus Christ was fully human. Born of a Jewish mother, He grew like other children. No one would have seen anything physically different about Jesus. In fact, He was so normal looking that His enemies had trouble picking Him out of a crowd.

8. Read Luke 2:52. What are the four areas of growth mentioned in this verse?

9. What are other evidences from the Gospels that Jesus had a human body?

For Jesus to become a man was a humbling experience that is beyond our comprehension. On earth, we see ourselves as the life form that is far superior to all other life forms. Who wouldn't want to be a human? But for Christ to take on the form of a man would be like a man taking on the form of a cockroach, except a lot lower. Humans certainly have value to God. After all, He created us in His image. But Christ is so superior to His creation that taking on the form of anything in creation takes more humility than we as humans can know.

10. Read Philippians 2:5–8. Once Christ became a man, He didn't stop humbling Himself. How did Christ humble Himself as a man?

Christ's humble mind-set serves as the example for us to follow (Phil. 2:5).

Messiah's Deity

Jesus Christ is also divine. He is the Son given by God (Isaiah 9:6; John 3:16). He lived on earth as the God-Man with absolute humanity and undiminished deity. This is a reality because of the Virgin Birth.

Jesus set aside the independent use of His attributes while He was on earth. He walked under the hot sun from city to city when He could have zapped Himself from place to place. He laid on the hard ground night after night when He could have snapped His fingers and had a room comparable to a suite at the Hilton. Jesus also could have anesthetized His body so He couldn't feel any pain at the Crucifixion. Instead, He felt the full brunt of the physical pain.

11. What else did Jesus endure because He humbly set aside His attributes?

Because of Jesus' humanity, He sympathizes with us; because of His deity, He can help us.

12. Read Hebrews 4:15 and 16. How is both Christ's deity and His humanity seen in this passage?

Messiah's Names

While Jesus' becoming a man was a humbling experience, it will ultimately mean His exaltation.

13. Read Philippians 2:9–11. How do these verses describe the name "Jesus?"

Isaiah listed the majestic names of Jesus that all will recognize after He returns a second time to set up His kingdom. "And his name shall be called Wonderful, Counsellor, The mighty God, The everlasting Father, The Prince of Peace" (v. 6). Every title given to the Messiah reveals His nature and being.

The title "Prince of Peace" often resonates with believers. This is perhaps one of His most celebrated titles. We sing of it in our hymns and Christmas music.

14. Read Matthew 10:34–36. What did Christ cause the first time He came to earth?

Christ did not bring peace at His first coming. Instead, He polarized people, and this polarization will continue until His second return (Matthew 10:34–36). Only when He returns the second time and establishes His kingdom will there be true peace. During the Millennium, when Christ reigns with His saints, there will be peace. In the meantime, He offers peace to the believer: "Therefore being justified by faith, we have peace with God through our Lord Jesus Christ" (Romans 5:1).

15. Which of the titles of the Messiah are particularly comforting to you?

Messiah's Rule

Isaiah prophesied concerning Messiah's reign, stating, "And the government shall be upon his shoulder" (Isaiah 9:6). Isaiah compared Messiah's governing responsibility to a kingly robe placed on His shoulder.

What right did Jesus Christ have to claim the throne of Israel? Isaiah explained the reasoning in verse 7.

The prophecy states that Messiah will sit upon the "throne of David, and upon his kingdom." God promised David that one of his "seed" would sit on his throne forever (2 Samuel 7:12–16). Isaiah also wrote of Messiah as "the stem of Jesse . . . a Branch . . . out of his roots" (Isaiah 11:1; cf. Revelation 5:5). Jesus Christ is the fulfillment of these prophecies. His legal right to David's throne came through Joseph, His legal (not biological) father, as recorded in Matthew 1. Jesus' right as the seed of David came through Mary, who was also of the line of David, as recorded in Luke 4.

Increase and peace will mark Messiah's kingdom: "Of the increase of His government and peace there shall be no end" (Isaiah 9:7). Daniel alluded to this idea in his interpretation of King Nebuchadnezzar's dream in which a multimetal image was destroyed by a stone. That stone then became a mountain filling the whole earth.

16. Read Daniel 2:44. What did Daniel write about the kingdom of Christ?

Peace will result, because Christ will rule. He will destroy all His enemies and bind Satan. Isaiah declared that the kingdom will be founded on principles of righteous judgment, "to order it, and to establish it with judgment and with justice."

Duration and Duration

Isaiah characterized the Lord's kingdom as having "no end." It would be "even for ever" (v. 7). Daniel made the same prediction (Daniel 7). But the Millennium will last for only a thousand years. Did the Bible contradict itself? No. Christ will reign for a thousand years. But He will then deliver up the Kingdom to the Father, and the reign will continue throughout eternity. Unlike the Assyrian, Babylonian, Persian, Greek, and Roman kingdoms, which faded from the scene as the next one arose, God's kingdom will last forever.

How will the Kingdom be achieved? Isaiah answered that question: "The zeal of the Lord of hosts will perform this" (Isaiah 9:7). Messiah's Kingdom will be a work of God. Israel will not overthrow some oppressing Gentile power to establish it. God will do it Himself. Daniel prophesied, "And in the days of these kings shall the God of heaven set up a kingdom, which shall never be destroyed; and the kingdom shall not be left to other people, but it shall break in pieces and consume all these kingdoms, and it shall stand forever" (Daniel 2:44).

Making It Personal

The humility of Christ accomplished the salvation of humans, but it also provided an example for us.

17. What evidences of humility would you like to see in your life?

Humility is the gateway to blessing before God. He is not impressed with who you are; He wants you to be impressed with Who He is. Rejoice in the opportunity to live humbly before God.

18. How will living humbly affect your life?

19. Memorize Isaiah 9:6 and 7.

Lesson 5

The Tenacious Twig

Christ is rejected by many people today as He was when He came to earth.

Isaiah 11:1, 2; 53:2; John 1

"For he shall grow up before him as a tender plant, and as a root out of a dry ground: he hath no form nor comeliness; and when we shall see him, there is no beauty that we should desire him" (Isaiah 53:2).

Over and over again we make poor decisions that make us scratch our heads in disbelief. Sometimes we can also be critical of the past decisions of others. The Jews rejected Jesus when He came to earth as their Messiah. It is easy to be critical of them, but we shouldn't think that we would have embraced Jesus if we had been in their place. We shouldn't forget that the majority of people still reject Christ today. Isaiah wrote about the humble beginnings of Jesus and the unlikely course He took in presenting Himself as the Messiah.

Getting Started

1. When was the last time you used poor judgment to make a decision that you later regretted?

2. What are some decisions by other people that have caused you to scratch your head in disbelief?

Searching the Scriptures

The last king of the Davidic dynasty to sit on the throne of Israel died nearly six hundred years before Jesus was born in Bethlehem. Zedekiah, the last reigning king, was carried captive to Babylon after his eyes had been gouged out (2 Kings 25:7). For the following six centuries, even after they returned to Judea following the Babylonian captivity, the Jews were dominated by Gentile kings. The people desperately needed a Messiah. But how would He appear?

Lowly Branch

Isaiah prophesied, "And there shall come forth a rod out of the stem of Jesse, and a Branch shall grow out of his roots" (Isaiah 11:1). The Hebrew word translated "roots" refers to the roots of a tree and also figuratively speaks of the permanence of God's people. Jesse was the father of King David. From the roots of David (his descendants) a twig would sprout up and grow. Verse 1 is a prophecy of Messiah's genealogical relationship to David.

During the six centuries following the fall of Jerusalem and the deposing of King Zedekiah, the Davidic dynasty lost its access to the throne. It was like a tree that had been chopped down but that had a live root awaiting an opportunity to send up a new shoot. The lifestyle of the royal family was reduced to that of the common peasant. Joseph was a lowly carpenter.

3. Read Luke 2:22–24 and Leviticus 12:2, 6–8. What does Joseph's offering say about the financial status of his family?

4. Read Matthew 8:20. When was the last time you heard a potential king admit that he was homeless?

After His crucifixion, a generous follower of Jesus laid Him in a borrowed grave (Matthew 27:60). Otherwise, He probably would have been put into a common grave.

Still, Jesus had the legal right to the throne. But He lacked the pomp associated with a throne, had no political support to place Him there, and had no goal to overthrow the Roman government. From the human standpoint, one can understand why the Jews were skeptical of Him. He just didn't look the part.

5. What would you expect to be the social and financial situation of a potential king?

6. What could a modern campaign manager suggest as a campaign slogan for Jesus just based on His social and financial situation?

Spirit-empowered

Jesus assumed the "form and fashion" of man (Philippians 2:7, 8), but His incarnation doesn't provide anyone with an excuse for rejecting Him. He had credentials given by the Holy Spirit. Isaiah wrote, "And the spirit of the Lord shall rest upon him, the spirit of wisdom and understanding, the spirit of counsel and might, the spirit of knowledge and of the fear of the Lord" (11:2). These characteristics would mark the Messiah. Isaiah presents the characteristics in pairs. The first characteristic in each pair is the source of the second one.

The spirit of wisdom is the ability to apply knowledge practically. Out of the spirit of wisdom comes the spirit of understanding, which is the ability to know right from wrong. Because of this, we can know that the Holy Spirit is omniscient.

The spirit of counsel is the ability to come to right conclusions. Out of the spirit of counsel comes the spirit of power. The spirit of power is the enablement to carry out the right conclusions. Thus, the Spirit is omnipotent.

The spirit of knowledge is the ability to know the essence of the Father. The Spirit knows God perfectly and therefore is God. Out of this knowledge comes a reverence for the things of God. So the Spirit is separate from God but still has the very essence of God.

7. How might a campaign manager change his slogan for Christ given the information about the Holy Spirit's anointing of Christ?

The Holy Spirit empowered Christ to perform miracles and cast out demons. When the Pharisees rejected the evidence and attributed His power to Satan, Christ warned them about committing the unpardonable sin of blaspheming the Spirit (Matthew 12:31, 32). The point is that while Christ's methods and manner reflected a mild and inauspicious person, His Spirit-empowered works demonstrated that He was all that He claimed to be.

Tender Plant

Continuing the symbolism of 11:1, in Isaiah 53:2, Isaiah wrote of the unbecoming appearance of the Messiah: "For he shall grow up before him as a tender plant, and as a root out of a dry ground."

8. Why is a "tender plant" a good picture of Christ?

The language in Isaiah 53:2 paints a picture of a plant struggling in a harsh, dry environment. It would be unusual to find a large, healthy plant flourishing in the middle of a desert. Isaiah used this symbolic picture to emphasize Christ's humble and unexpected beginning.

9. Why is a "dry ground" a good illustration of the political and spiritual environment of Israel at the time of Christ?

The spiritual and political conditions of Jesus' day were not what one might expect for a Savior-King announced by heavenly hosts.

On the other hand, could there have been a setting in which a Savior-King was more greatly needed? God delights in meeting man's deepest needs in unusual and unexpected ways.

10. What are some examples of unlikely people that God to do mighty works?

Isaiah compared Christ to the tender plant and root from the dry ground to explain the unbelief implied in the previous question: "Who hath believed our report?" (53:1). The implied answer is that no one had believed the report, because of Christ's unlikely and unpromising beginning.

Undesirable Appearance

11. What is your reaction when you see pictures of Christ with a halo over His head and a glow around His handsome face?

12. Read Isaiah 53:2. What is the accurate picture of Jesus' appearance?

Jesus was rejected partially because He looked like a common man. Nothing about Jesus' physical appearance drew people to Him. Most likely, Christ was a very plain, ordinary looking man. He did not stand head and shoulders above the crowd, as did Saul. Nor did he have the physical strength of Samson or the beauty of Absalom. If there were such a thing as a generic-looking Jew, He was one. The point is that His physical appearance alone did not attract others to Him.

The people of Jesus' day should have looked beyond the physical and looked to the Scripture to see if Jesus fulfilled the Messianic prophecies. They should have looked at the miraculous works He did.

13. Read Matthew 10:37 and 38. What did Jesus challenge His critics to do?

The Jews had a reason for rejecting Jesus, but it was unjustifiable. Everyone who rejects the Lord as Savior has a reason for doing so, but these reasons will not stand before the Judge of all the earth.

Unfortunate Response

Israel rejected her Messiah at His first coming. This rejection becomes clear as one reads the Gospels. John's opening words indicate the reasons Christ should not have been rejected.

14. Read John 1:1–14.Based on these verses, what are five reasons Christ should not have been rejected?

Jesus is eternal. He is God. He made all things (John 1:1–3). This eternal One became incarnate and lived among His people. He revealed His glory to them (v. 14). Israel had no acceptable reason for rejecting this gracious and truthful One.

Still, Israel did reject Him. John wrote, “He was in the world, and the world was made by him, and the world knew him not. He came unto his own, and his own received him not” (vv. 10, 11).

Rejected Today

Not only did the Jews reject Messiah at His first coming, but they continue to do so today.

15. Why do people reject Christ today?

Paul addressed the Jews’ rejection of Christ in the book of Romans. While the majority have rejected Him, Paul quoted Isaiah to prove that “a remnant shall be saved” (Romans 9:27). Paul further demonstrated that God has not completely set Israel aside, for “at this present time also there is a remnant according to the election of grace,” and he used himself as an example of God’s continuing work with Israel (Romans 11:1–5). He also argued that not only was Israel’s blindness “in part” but also temporary, for the day will come when “all Israel shall be saved” (Romans 11:25, 26). This salvation will come to Israel when the Lord returns at His Second Coming (Zechariah 12:10).

The Gospels record a small number of Gentiles who sought Him. When the church began, it was entirely Jewish; but by the end of Paul’s missionary ministry, it was largely Gentile. Today, most who respond to the gospel message are Gentiles. However, the vast majority continue to reject Him today. Paul taught that the setting aside of the Jews was part of God’s divine plan that He might provide salvation for the Gentiles (Romans 11:11–13.)

Making It Personal

16. What are some ways a believer might reject Christ?

Outwardly appearing to accept Christ fully should not be our focus. We should make sure that we have not rejected Christ in the most secretive and private areas of our lives.

17. Invite Christ into every area of your life. Embrace Him fully.

18. Memorize Isaiah 53:2.

Lesson 6

Messiah's Message, Ministry, and Miracles

The compassion Christ showed at His first coming was a precursor to the compassion He will show at His Second Coming.

Isaiah 61:1, 2; 42:1–7; 35:3–6

"Behold my servant, whom I uphold; mine elect, in whom my soul delighteth; I have put my spirit upon him: he shall bring forth judgment to the Gentiles" (Isaiah 42:1).

One day a homeless man was walking down a sidewalk in a nice, suburban neighborhood. He was in the neighborhood because it was trash day and he was hungry. When he stopped to dig through the trash of one particular house, the man living in the house spotted him from his kitchen. Instead of shooing the homeless man away or calling the police, the homeowner began to make a sandwich for him. By the time he finished, the homeless man was gone. Instead of giving up, the homeowner drove his car around until he found the homeless man and gave him the sandwich.

The homeowner had compassion on the needy man, and his compassion moved him to act. Christ was also a compassionate minister while He was on earth. His compassion for people serves as our example.

Getting Started

1. What is the first word that comes to your mind when you hear the word "compassion"?

2. What displays of compassion have you witnessed?

Searching the Scriptures

Old Testament prophecies commonly made no distinction between the first and the second coming of Messiah. The prophets did not realize that an extended period of time (at least two thousand years) would elapse between Christ's sacrificial work and His sovereign reign.

3. Read 1 Peter 1:10–12. What did Peter write about the prophet's perspective on the comings of Christ?

Unlike the prophets, Jesus knew the timetable for His ministry.

Message of Deliverance

Isaiah 61:1–3 contains prophecies about Christ's first coming and His second coming. Verse one and first part of verse two were fulfilled during Christ's first coming. The second part of verse 2 and verse 3 refer to events that Christ will fulfill at His second coming. In Luke 4:16–22, Christ claimed the fulfillment of the prophecy of Isaiah 61:1 and 2a.

4. Read Isaiah 61:1. What characterized the people on whom Jesus focused His ministry?

Jesus did indeed "preach good tidings unto the meek" (Isaiah 61:1). The word "gospel," used in the Luke 4 account, literally means good news or good tidings. Jesus healed the "brokenhearted," those who recognize their sin, repent, and turn to the Lord. Jesus was always tender toward those who were hurting.

5. Read Mark 6:34. What is Jesus communicating about Himself by characterizing the brokenhearted as "sheep not having a shepherd"?

Jesus ministered to the spiritual needs of the brokenhearted by teaching them. Paul instructed the believers of Thessalonica to "comfort the feebleminded," or literally "encourage the fainthearted" (1 Thessalonians 5:14). Those who claim to follow Jesus should exhibit the caring, compassionate spirit the Lord Jesus exemplified.

Messiah was predicted "to proclaim liberty to the captive, and the opening of the prison to them that are bound" (Isaiah 61:1). Satan holds sinful man captive. Paul wrote of those "who are taken captive by him at his will" (2 Timothy 2:26). Christ came to free the sinner.

Messiah was also "to proclaim the acceptable year of the Lord." Of the fifty-six times that the word "acceptable" occurs in the Old Testament, fifteen times it is translated "favour."

Message of Judgment

The "day of vengeance" (Isaiah 61:2b) speaks of the judgments that will take place at the Second Coming.

6. Read 2 Thessalonians 1:7–9. What does Paul write about the intensity of the judgments associated with Christ's Second Coming?

Several judgments will be associated with the Lord's Second Coming. Israel will be judged, and the rebellious will be purged (Ezekiel 20:35–38). Likewise, Christ will judge living Gentiles in the valley of Jehoshaphat, where He will separate them as a shepherd separates his sheep and goats. Christ will then command that the unsaved (goats) be cast into the Lake of Fire (Joel 3:2–17; Matthew 25:31–46).

Message of Comfort

The Second Coming will be not only a time of judgment but also a time of comfort for those who have turned to Christ. Isaiah declared that Christ would "comfort all that mourn" (Isaiah 61: 3). During the Tribulation, many will mourn their sin and receive Christ as their Savior. Specifically, Christ will give "beauty for ashes" to the mourners at His Second Coming. "Beauty" refers to a headdress worn at times of rejoicing. "Ashes" were symbolic of mourning. Jews put the headdresses and ashes on their heads as outward symbols of their inward feelings.

Anointing someone with oil was a way of demonstrating joy. Christ used this symbol to expand on the idea of His ministry to the mourning.

The mourning will also be able to shed their "spirit of heaviness" for figurative "garments of praise." And instead of mourning, they will become like fruitful trees that bring glory to the Lord.

7. What are some events of the Tribulation that would most certainly traumatize the people who live through them? (See Revelation 8:7—9:21.)

Christ's comfort of those who turned to Him during the Tribulation will be complete.

Justice and Humility

Considering the fanfare that characterizes political campaigns today, Jesus' grassroots approach seems rather low-key. Political analysts would probably conclude that He was destined to fail because He didn't use successful campaigning methods. Remember that Jesus presented Himself as the King of Israel.

Matthew 12:18 quotes Isaiah 42:1 and applies it to Christ. He will, the verse declares, bring judgment (justice) to the Gentiles. Messiah's ministry, then, will establish a just judgment and will include the Gentiles. But until Christ's millennial rule, we will continue to face a world filled with injustice and inequality.

An endorsement from a prominent figure always helps a political candidate. Jesus Christ had the endorsement of God the Father, who said of Jesus on two separate occasions, "I am well pleased" (Matthew 3:17; 17:5). If you've ever seen a political convention on TV, you know that as soon as a candidate is nominated, his or her followers react with a loud, orchestrated demonstration. Jesus Christ did not use loud, overbearing tactics. He did "not cry, nor lift up, nor cause his voice to be heard in the street." Rather, He let His teaching, healing, and caring ministry speak for itself.

8. Read Matthew 20:25–28. How did Christ characterize His ministry in this passage?

Isaiah referred to Messiah as "my servant" (42:1). Jesus exemplified the model of a humble servant. Emphasize that every believer should pursue this characteristic.

Gentle Ministry

A former American president made the slogan, "a kinder, gentler nation," part of his campaign platform. Whether he produced that quality in his four years of office remains a matter of debate. But there is no question that Christ Jesus was kind and gentle. The "bruised reed" and the "smoking flax" refer to the poor, the downtrodden, the needy. Christ came to minister to those people (cf. Matthew 9:10–13). He was a "friend of . . . sinners" (Matthew 11:19). Likewise, Christians should be willing to associate with those who are of a lower class.

9. What excuses might believers give for not reaching out to those who are downtrodden and needy?

Successful Ministry

Isaiah 42:4 promises Messiah will ultimately be victorious. Jesus lost His initial bid to be king of Israel and His opponents crucified Him. Yet He will not be "discouraged," for He will someday be not only the King of Israel, but also the "King of kings, and Lord of lords" (Revelation 19:16).

The great Creator of the heavens and earth commissioned Messiah "in righteousness" (Isaiah 42:6), meaning He gave Messiah the responsibility of doing God's righteous will. Christ always did the will of the Father. God's will for Him extended beyond Israel to all of creation. He would fulfill God's covenant promises with Israel and at the same time be a light to the Gentiles. Gentiles have come to trust in Him, and He will have a continued ministry with the Gentiles throughout the Millennium. John prophesied of a time when "the kingdoms of this world are become the kingdoms of our Lord, and of his Christ; and he shall reign for ever and ever" (Revelation 11:15).

At the first coming of Christ, Jesus performed many miracles. He gave the blind their sight. But He also brought spiritual sight to those blinded by Satan (2 Corinthians 4:4). He freed sinners from the bondage of sin. To all who trust Him, He brings release, sight and light. When He establishes His kingdom, He will bring both physical and spiritual deliverance to Gentiles as well as to Jews.

10. Evaluate the following statement: Showing compassion to those with physical needs is not important to Christ today since helping a person's physical body does not affect the destiny of his or her soul.

Miracles as Credentials

Jesus performed miracles to authenticate His message. Nicodemus recognized this purpose when he remarked, "Rabbi, we know that thou art a teacher come from God: for no man can do these miracles that thou doest, except God be with him" (John 3:2). Matthew's statement that Jesus spoke with authority (Matthew 7:29) is followed by two chapters recording ten of His miracles. They demonstrated His authority (Matthew 9:6). Isaiah prophesied of the miracles Messiah would perform, miracles that would act as His credentials.

Isaiah 35 is a prophecy of the millennial Kingdom and its physical and spiritual blessings. The kingdom encompasses all peoples and all the earth. But the passage is not limited to the future kingdom, for a portion of it is quoted in the New Testament and applied to the ministry of Christ. When John, who was languishing in prison, sent messengers to ask Jesus whether He was indeed the "coming one" (Matthew 11:2, 3), Jesus replied by pointing to His works.

The Coming One in Matthew 11:4 is a clear reference to Messiah. Jesus' credentials were that He was fulfilling the Messianic job description given by Isaiah.

Matthew's summary statement is worth quoting: "And great multitudes came unto him, having with them those that were lame, blind, dumb, maimed, and many others, and cast them down at Jesus' feet; and he healed them: insomuch that the multitude wondered, when they saw the dumb to speak, the maimed to be whole, the lame to walk, and the blind to see: and they glorified the God of Israel" (15:30, 31).

The Lord also intended His miracles to cause others to have faith in Himself as the Son of God. John stated his purpose in choosing the miracles which he recorded.

11. Read John 20:31. What was John's purpose in recording the miracles of Jesus in his gospel?

In several instances, faith is mentioned as one of the outcomes of a miracle. But note that miracles alone never produced faith. Many who saw His miracles were merely entertained, or they simply discounted the significance of the miracles.

Christ's miracles also illustrated His kind, compassionate character. Hurting people deeply moved Him, and He sought always to minister to the needy.

Miracles as Illustrations

In many ways, the physical healings Jesus performed were intended to illustrate the spiritual healing He offered, a healing that will be completely fulfilled with the institution of the millennial Kingdom. Isaiah wrote, "And in that day shall the deaf hear the words of the book, and the eyes of the blind shall see out of obscurity, and out of darkness" (29:18). Isaiah was not speaking of physical healing but of the spiritual healing during Messiah's kingdom and of the people's response to the words of Messiah rather than to the works of Messiah.

Jesus' miracles foreshadowed conditions during the Millennium. Jesus began His ministry announcing, "Repent: for the kingdom of heaven is at hand" (Matthew 4:17). He drew around Him a few loyal supporters, campaigned throughout Galilee proclaiming His message, and worked all kinds of miracles among the people (Matthew 4:18–25). The miracles served as the candidate's record, and they demonstrated that what He did on a limited local level He could do on a national and universal level when Israel receives Him as her rightful king. During the Millennium, sickness will be banished, hunger abolished, and sin with its binding power will be curtailed. Satan will be bound and, therefore, unable to deceive people. People will experience prosperity and longevity. The miracles of the first advent are a foretaste of what God has in store for the world when Christ becomes King of Kings and Lord of Lords.

12. Which physical diseases are you personally looking forward to seeing Christ abolish at His Second Coming?

13. How does the prospect of a glorified body free from all sickness and disease help you to deal with physical ailments now?

Making It Personal

14. What part should compassion play in your witnessing efforts?

15. Which should come first, presenting the gospel to the lost or compassionately ministering to their needs?

16. Recognize Christ as your example of compassion for both the needy and the lost. Look for opportunities to show compassion to both groups this week.

17. Memorize Isaiah 42:1.

Lesson 7

The Might and Magnificence of Messiah

The Messiah-God is great.

Isaiah 40:1–31

"He shall feed his flock like a shepherd: he shall gather the lambs with his arm, and carry them in his bosom, and shall gently lead those that are with young" (Isaiah 40:11).

What separates a superhero from a villain in comic books? What makes people cheer for Superman, Spiderman, and Batman and boo the Green Goblin, the Joker, and the Riddler? The difference in how people respond to them has nothing to do with which powers they possess. The difference is in what they do with their powers. The Superheroes are super because they help people. They use their abilities compassionately.

In the real world, people often trample on others on their way to gaining power. In essence, they are playing the part of the villain. Christ has power that infinitely surpasses the power of any person. Yet, He uses His power compassionately.

Getting Started

1. What three names would you include in a list of powerful people?

2. Which of the powerful people in your list would you also consider as a person of compassion?

3. Why is it necessary for Christ to be both powerful and compassionate?

Searching the Scripture

Chapter 40 begins the second section of the book of Isaiah. The first thirty-nine chapters deal with a denunciation of Israel's sins. The last twenty-seven chapters address restoration and deliverance after her punishment. Remember that Isaiah wrote these chapters a century before Babylon took Judah captive. In this last section, Isaiah anticipated the nation's captivity and her restoration seventy years later, and he wrote to encourage the people of Judah in their walk with God.

Pardon Promise

In Isaiah 40:1 and 2 God offered comfort to Judah; He referred to them as "my people." Despite their sin, He hadn't forgotten them. Even during the captivity (which at that time was still in the future), He graciously remembered the covenant relationship He had with Israel. Thus Isaiah spoke "comfortably" to (literally, "to the heart of") Jerusalem (v. 2).

4. Read Isaiah 40:2. What was God's message of comfort to Israel?

God had completed His disciplinary action against Israel. The years of captivity had been like the hardships of war, but now "her warfare is accomplished."

The Babylonian captivity had not come without warning. Years earlier, God had warned that if Judah disobeyed Him, she would be punished, even cast out of the land (Deuteronomy 28:15–68). Isaiah saw that God would indeed render and finish this punishment. The phrase "her iniquity is pardoned" shows that Israel would have a change of heart while in captivity and would turn back to God. Along with Isaiah, Jeremiah also predicted that God would look favorably on His people.

Scholars differ over the meaning of "she hath received of the Lord's hand double for all her sins" (Isaiah 40:2). Some think it means that God doubly punished Israel; some think it means that the nation was "sufficiently" punished. Others see it as the punishment she suffered in captivity and the suffering Christ endured as her sin-bearer.

Preparation for God's Coming

To illustrate Israel's return from Babylon, Isaiah makes an analogy of road building: hills cut down, low spots graded in, obstacles removed, curves straightened out (Isaiah 40:3, 4).

5. Read Isaiah 40:3 and 4. How is this passage used in the New Testament? (See Matthew 3:1–3.)

6. Why is clearing a path and laying a smooth highway a good illustration of what it took to bring Judah back from captivity and restore them to their land?

God showed both His providential power and His love and concern when He brought Judah back to their land. The road was impossible until God intervened and made it happen. Nehemiah witnessed first hand the powerful and compassionate work of God.

7. Read Nehemiah 1. How are both God's power and compassion seen in Nehemiah's prayer about the rebuilding of Jerusalem?

Isaiah 40:5 speaks of a day when "the glory of the Lord" would be "revealed" to "all flesh." John wrote, "We beheld his glory" when "the Word became flesh" (John 1:14). Christ's ultimate glory will be seen in the millennial Kingdom. The Transfiguration, witnessed by Peter, James and John, was a preview of that glory (Matthew 16:28—17:9; see also 2 Peter 1:16–18).

Eternal Word

In Isaiah 40:6–8, Isaiah contrasted man's temporal, transient existence with God's eternal, enduring Word. The Jews in exile could take comfort in knowing that the Babylonian power was temporary. Because God's Word is eternal, these prophecies would be fulfilled.

The situation the exiles faced was virtually hopeless. They couldn't imagine ever becoming a nation again. But God's Word about their return to the land couldn't be squelched by Babylon, the superpower of that time.

8. When have you clung to promises in God's Word when all seemed hopeless?

Isaiah 40:9–11 announced the good tidings to the Judean towns: God was their sovereign. "Behold your God!" (v. 9). Look to Him is the announcement. Don't let the dire circumstances around you make you afraid. What a bright message of hope in a dark hour for Judah.

Isaiah may have assumed that Messiah would establish His reign immediately after the Jews returned from captivity (vv. 10, 11). However, Scripture written later reveals that there will be an extended time before the messianic Kingdom.

9. Read Isaiah 40:10 and 11. In what contrasting ways does God use His arms and hands in these two verses?

Majestic Creator

Isaiah acknowledged that God created the heavens and the earth. By asking some rhetorical questions, he illustrated God's superiority over both the natural universe and humanity. Isaiah wrote that God created and controls all things.

The Lord created the heaven and the earth with no help from anyone. Using anthropomorphic language, Isaiah pictured Him scooping up the water for the seas with His hands, measuring the heavens with the span and weighing out dust in balance scales for mountains (Isaiah 40:12–14). Regardless of how majestic and huge the creation is, God is more grand and illustrious.

10. What do you find to be the most amazing fact about the size or complexity of God's creation?

In verse 13, the question "Who hath directed the Spirit of the Lord, or being his counsellor hath taught him?" teaches about God's wisdom. God needs no counselor, as humans do (see Proverbs 11:14). His wisdom, knowledge, and might are sufficient.

God has never had a counselor or teacher (Isaiah 40:14). For a man to be untaught and without instruction makes him ignorant. But with God, it only further proves His intelligence. No man, no matter how wise, has the least thing to offer God. He is the source of all wisdom.

God created not only the earth but its inhabitants as well. Today we classify nations from "emerging nations" to the "superpowers," but in God's sight they are all insignificant (v. 15).

11. Rub your finger along a surface where dust has collected and look at the dust collected on your finger. What does God compare to a layer of dust in Isaiah 40:15?

The mightiest nations with their wealth, political power and military might are to God no more than the drops of water that drip from a bucket as it is lifted from a well. They are no more than minuscule dust particles on the scales.

And all the commodities and goods a nation can produce are insufficient (v. 16) for a worthy sacrifice to Him. Lebanon, noted for its mighty cedar trees, had neither sufficient wood for a fire nor beasts for an offering.

The Creation of Gods

One of life's greatest ironies is that man, who was created in God's own image, refused to worship his Creator and instead chose to worship gods patterned after man himself, with all his sinful passions and weaknesses. Conveniently, these human-like gods don't hold man morally responsible.

12. Read Isaiah 40:18–20. Evaluate the following statement: The worship of idols is at its core an attempt to manipulate a supernatural power.

Uncivilized pagans fashion gods from wood, stone, bone, or metal; civilized, educated pagans fashion gods from the thoughts and ideas of the mind. A poor man, who can't afford a rich image made of silver or gold, must worship one carved from wood. But this idol is no more foolish than a rich man's idol.

God challenges mankind to make an honest comparison: "To whom then will ye liken God? or what likeness will ye compare unto him?" (v. 18).

Israel's worship of idols was one of the sins that led to her captivity. But in Babylon, the mother of idolatry, Israel got her fill of idolatry and never had a problem with it thereafter. In Babylon, the Jews learned the folly of worshiping idols. They would therefore understand Isaiah's description of an idol in verse 19, realizing that even one made of gold and silver could not compare to God.

Mighty Controller

Not only is God the creator of the universe, He is also the controller (Isaiah 40:21–26). Isaiah asked four rhetorical questions, questions that seem to say, "Don't you all know this?" From the creation of man (even before God chose Israel as His people) man had knowledge of God. Adam, the father of humanity, knew the Creator-God. Noah, the father of the present nations of the world, knew this same God. It is not God's fault that men do not know Him today. Man has rejected a knowledge of Him, replacing Him with man-made idols. Still, He controls the universe that He created.

It is understandable that Isaiah devoted so much of the text to emphasizing both God's power and His care for His people. While in captivity, the Jews may have wondered where God was. Had He abandoned them? Could He do anything for them in Babylon? But Isaiah reassured Israel that the Most High God was active and well in Babylon.

Isaiah pictured God as a governor sitting on the circle of the earth and its human inhabitants as mere grasshoppers (v. 22).

13. What do you learn about people by comparing them to grasshoppers?

God controls man; princes and rulers are under His jurisdiction, and He demotes them at His will (v. 23). Isaiah 40:24 emphasizes how short the reign of earthly kings is.

14. Read Isaiah 40:23 and 24. How should these verses affect politicians?

Using language that his readers could have easily grasped, Isaiah compared God's dwelling to a vast tent made of the outstretched heavens (v. 22). Verse 25, which God spoke, repeats the challenge of verse 18, which Isaiah spoke. Who is equal to God? A look at the starry sky reveals God's splendor and man's insignificance. God created the stars and named each one of them (cf. Genesis 1:14; Amos 5:8; Job 38:31–33).

15. When was the last time you gazed into the heavens on a clear night away from city lights? What goes through your mind when you see all those stars?

Mindful Caretaker

God is not limited to one task at a time. Isaiah 40:27 anticipates a complaint from God's people who thought that God had forgotten them (the long years of captivity to come might cause some to think this). Although the Northern Kingdom was taken into captivity by the Assyrians more than a century before the Southern Kingdom was taken captive by Babylon, God never forgot His people or the covenants He had made with them (cf. Psalm 121:3, 4).

The questions of verse 28 begin like those of verse 21. "Doesn't everybody know?"

16. Read Isaiah 40:28. When, if ever, have you felt like God was asleep on the job?

17. How does this verse encourage you?

God has strength not only to complete His work but also to enable His people to complete the return to Jerusalem (vv. 29–31). The journey would be tiring, and though they might faint, God would renew their strength.

Making It Personal

18. Spend a few moments meditating on the greatness of God. Reread Isaiah 40:12–17.

19. In light of God's power and greatness, take you the difficulties and struggles you are facing to the Lord in prayer.

20. Memorize Isaiah 40:11.

Lesson 8

The Unjust Suffering of Messiah

Christ suffered an unjust, agonizing death.

Isaiah 52:13—53:12

"But he was wounded for our transgressions, he was bruised for our iniquities: the chastisement of our peace was upon him; and with his stripes we are healed" (Isaiah 53:5).

All of us experience unfair treatment from time to time, and we all bristle when it happens. No one likes being treated unfairly. The rise in lawsuits is evidence of that.

Christ endured unspeakable suffering, torture, and pain—none of which He deserved—to save us from our sin. His unjust suffering is the focus of this study.

Getting Started

1. When have you experienced something that you believed to be unfair?

2. How did you respond?

Searching the Scriptures

This study and the following two studies are based on Isaiah 52:13—53:12. Therefore, some of the verses and the messages will overlap. This lesson will emphasize Christ's unjust suffering at the Crucifixion. Lesson 9 will stress that Christ suffered for us as our substitute. Lesson 10 will focus on the result of this suffering.

The verses in Isaiah 52:13—53:12 form a unit, a song about the Suffering Servant, comprised of five sections, or stanzas, of three verses each: Messiah's preeminence (52:13–15), His person (53:1–3), His passion (53:4–6), His passivity (53:7–9) and His portion (53:10–13).

No other passage in the Old Testament comes close to describing the suffering of the Messiah so completely as Isaiah 53. The individual words used are strong and picturesque. Isaiah wrote the first three verses of that chapter from the perspective of a Jew considering the crucifixion after he had come to understand what had actually happened.

Messiah's suffering was not limited to the beating, the scourging, and the actual crucifixion. He suffered in other ways too.

Social Suffering

Christ's social suffering began long before His crucifixion. The people's rejection caused Him social and mental anguish.

3. What do you know about being rejected socially?

4. When have you had someone turn on you or refuse to recognize you as a friend?

Unbelief characterized many people's responses toward Christ (53:1). His unbecoming appearance did not draw men to Him (53:2).

5. Read John 1:46. What did Nathanael say that represented a prevailing thought in Jesus' day?

When challenged by Nicodemus to give Him a fair hearing, the leaders replied, "Out of Galilee ariseth no prophet" (John 7:52). People despised and rejected Him (Isaiah 53:3). Isaiah wrote that they hid their faces from Him—a phrase used to describe turning away from a leper. Christians sing about the Man of Sorrows with joyful, thankful hearts. But those who saw Him experiencing those sorrows had no loving gratitude in their hearts. To them, He was a failure.

Physical Suffering

6. Read Isaiah 52:14. To what extreme was Jesus marred?

7. When Christ was on the cross, do you think He looked as peaceful as many artists have depicted Him? Why or why not?

Isaiah 52:14 is a summary statement concerning the despicable suffering Christ experienced. He endured such punishment that onlookers were awestruck by His appearance. They found it amazing that one who suffered so much could be exalted and honored. His "visage" (outward appearance) was "marred" beyond recognition. However, through His suffering He became the perfect sacrifice for sin. It has been suggested that Christ suffered more on the cross than any other human being has ever suffered.

In Isaiah 53:5, Isaiah wrote that Christ was "wounded," referring to a piercing wound made by a sword or spear. Jesus' hands and feet were pierced with spikes (John 20:25), and a soldier pierced his side with a spear (John 19:34). These wounds to Christ's body will remain visible throughout eternity, as implied when John saw a "Lamb as it had been slain" (Revelation 5:6).

8. What do you think you will say when you meet Jesus and notice the scars on His hands and feet?

"The chastisement of our peace was upon him" (Isaiah 53:5). Chastisement refers to disciplinary punishment. God gave the punishment due us to Him when He became our substitutionary sacrifice.

"With his stripes we are healed" (53:5). The stripes are the wounds left by a whip laced with sharp metal pieces. The scourging Christ faced at the hands of the Roman soldiers left His back striped with raw, open lacerations. Pieces of sharp metal and stone pierced His back with each stinging blow of the whip. The metal then tore through His flesh as the whipped was pulled across His back.

Jesus was also "oppressed and afflicted" (53:7). A form of the word "oppressed" is found in Exodus 5, where it is translated "taskmaster." Under the oppressive hand of Pharaoh, taskmasters forced the Israelites to work as slaves, suffering physical beating and perilous working conditions. The word "afflicted" (see also verse 4) is sometimes translated "humble" and includes the thought of browbeating. It is an apt picture of the way the Romans and the Jews treated Christ.

Emotional Suffering

Men misunderstood Christ's mission and the cause of His suffering. At first reading, it would seem that the phrase "He was bruised for our iniquities" (53:5; cf. v. 10) refers to physical suffering. But the word "bruised" actually means crushed or destroyed as an enemy in battle. From other usages of the word, we can see that Isaiah was speaking figuratively of oppressive mental and emotional suffering rather than of physical abuse. In verse 12, we read that while on the cross, Jesus Christ "was numbered with the transgressors"; that is, He was counted as, or considered to be, a transgressor. He would have been buried with the two thieves who were crucified with Him if a wealthy man had not intervened and provided his own tomb.

For Christ, the most painful part of the entire crucifixion experience was most likely when God the Father "laid on him the iniquity of us all" (Isaiah 53:6) and made His soul "an offering for sin" (vv. 10–12). The sins of the world were placed on Him.

9. Read Isaiah 53:6. How should Christ's anguish of bearing the world's sin on the cross affect your desire to sin?

When Christ prayed, "O my Father, if it be possible, let this cup pass from me" (Matthew 26:39), He was not seeking to avoid the physical suffering of the cross but the spiritual separation from God caused by being made sin. His cry of anguish, "My God, My God, why hast thou forsaken me?" (Matthew 27:46), further reflects the suffering of separation from God.

10. Read Matthew 27:46. What is the answer to Jesus' question?

While this passage from Isaiah emphasizes Messiah's suffering, it is His death that provides justification. Suffering alone, no matter how severe, couldn't have bought our redemption. It was Christ's death that paid sin's penalty (Acts 17:3; 1 Corinthians 15:3).

Unjust Suffering

Some people deserve the punishment they suffer, because they either sinned or did some foolish deed. But Christ did not deserve to suffer. He neither sinned nor acted foolishly. His innocence is illustrated in the figure of a "lamb [brought] to the slaughter, and as a sheep before her shearers" (Isaiah 53:7). Isaiah proclaimed Messiah's innocence.

11. Read Isaiah 53:9 and 11. How is Jesus' innocence seen in these verses?

Jesus was taken in His prime (about age thirty-three). He had no descendants, as Isaiah implied: "Who shall declare his generation?" (Isaiah 53:8). The Jews considered it a tragic fate to die childless, for who would carry on the family name? Yet Messiah will have a "seed" (v. 10), those who are born again by His redemptive work.

Trial Irregularities

Christ faced additional injustices during His trial. The trial included false witnesses (Matthew 26:60) and statements taken out of context (v. 61). He was struck before being found guilty (John 18:22). Contrary to the laws of justice, the witnesses against Him did not appear personally before Pilate (John 18:28). The Roman government scourged, mocked, and crucified Christ even though they had found no fault in Him (19:1–4). Pilate, who declared Him innocent, succumbed to the Jews' demands and let Jesus be crucified (v. 16).

Isaiah predicted this injustice: "He was taken from prison and from judgment" (Isaiah 53:8).

12. Why didn't Christ declare a mistrial and demand that He be tried again?

As Jesus Christ stood bound before His accusers, He found no justice. He was taken away to be crucified. In actuality, there was no legal way for Christ to be found worthy of the death penalty.

13. Read 1 Peter 3:18. According to Peter, why was it impossible to find Jesus guilty and worthy of death?

Divine justice called for the satisfaction of a Holy God, which could be accomplished only as that Holy God Himself provided the perfect sacrifice.

Christ could have prayed for "twelve legions of angels" to defend Him (Matthew 26:53), but He chose not to. Why? Because He knew that His death had a purpose. He chose to give His life (John 10:17), as a "good shepherd giveth his life for the sheep" (v. 11).

Erroneous Conclusions

These haunting questions remain: Why was the Lord Jesus Christ treated so badly? Was He not recognized as a man who went about "doing good" (Acts 10:38)? Why would anyone want to harm such an admirable person?

As men looked at the grief heaped upon the Messiah, they saw only the physical suffering. They assumed that He had brought it on Himself, that He had sinned, and that as a result, God was punishing Him (Isaiah 53:4). The people mocked Jesus, assuming that if He truly were God's Son, God would deliver him from the cross (Matthew 27:41–44). The Jews believed they were serving God by putting Christ to death.

Jesus' crucifiers looked at the credentials from Heaven and concluded that they were from Hell. Because they misunderstood who He was, they misunderstood why He suffered. They did not recognize that He was suffering for them.

14. Read Luke 23:34. What did Christ request of the Father that showed the ignorance of His accusers?

Eternal Plan

The Crucifixion did not take God by surprise. Speaking to the men of Israel, Peter proclaimed: "Him [Christ], being delivered by the determinate counsel and foreknowledge of God, ye have taken, and by wicked hands have crucified and slain" (Acts 2:23). Notice the delicate balance between God's sovereign plan and man's responsibility. The words "wicked hands" show that Peter held the Jews responsible for Christ's death, even though it was part of the eternal divine plan.

15. Read Revelation 13:8. What does this passage say about Jesus that shows His death was part of God's plan?

From God's perspective, the suffering of Christ was completed in eternity past. Simply stated, the suffering and crucifixion of Christ were all part of God's eternal plan. Therefore, Isaiah could clearly prophesy of it centuries before it happened: "Yet it pleased the Lord to bruise him; he hath put him to grief" (Isaiah 53:10), and "the Lord hath laid on him the iniquity of us all" (v. 6).

Why was Jesus Christ, the Messiah, put to such abuse? Because it was part of God's redemptive plan for sinful man, an act of God's love. This is the background for the most popular of Bible verses: "For God so loved the world, that he gave his only begotten Son, that whosoever believeth in him should not perish, but have everlasting life" (John 3:16).

Making It Personal

16. What causes you to say, "I deserve better"?

17. Have you ever said that because of how people treated you while you were ministering? If so, when?

Keep the example of Christ in mind as you serve. Do it with the selfless, sacrificial attitude that Christ had when He unjustly went to the cross for us.

18. Memorize Isaiah 53:5.

Lesson 9

The Vicarious Suffering of Messiah

Messiah suffered as our substitute.

Isaiah 52:13—53:12

"All we like sheep have gone astray; we have tuned every one to his own way; and the LORD hath laid on him the iniquity of us all" (Isaiah 53:6).

The use of sugar to sweeten food goes back many years. But, using sugar substitutes has been a more recent phenomenon. Sweet 'n Low, Splenda, and NutraSweet are just three of the sugar substitutes that have come along over the years. The benefit of the substitutes is that they have less calories. Their drawback is that they don't taste quite as good as sugar. None of the sugar substitutes are as sweet as sugar.

When we speak of Jesus as our Substitute, we don't mean that He is an inferior Substitute. He is the perfect Substitute who did for us what we could never do ourselves.

Getting Started

1. What is your favorite sugar substitute?

2. What sugar substitutes have you used over your lifetime?

3. How does a substitute usually compare to the original?

4. How does Jesus Christ, your Substitute, compare to you?

Searching the Scripture

This is the second of three studies on Isaiah 53. Lesson 8 centered on the terrible physical and emotional suffering that Christ endured. This week's lesson focuses on the Messiah as the substitute for sin.

If Christ suffered and died as man's substitute, the logical question to ask is, Why was it necessary? Why did man need a substitute?

Origin of Sin

People need a substitute to pay the penalty for their sins because they cannot pay the penalty themselves. Every person is a sinner both by nature and by deed. How did we become sinners? Did God create us this way? No, God did not create us as a sinner. God's creation, including man, was good.

Sin originated within the angelic realm when Lucifer chose to rebel against God and refused the high but subordinate position God assigned to him.

5. Read Isaiah 14:12–14 and Ezekiel 28:12–19. What was Satan's root sin?

Satan's choice to sin apparently occurred early in the creative process, for John wrote of him, "He was a murderer from the beginning. . . . When he speaketh a lie, he speaketh of his own: for he is a liar, and the father of it" (John 8:44). Genesis 3:4 contains the first recorded lie of Satan. He questioned Eve and then plainly denied God's word.

6. Read Genesis 3:4. What was Satan's lie to Eve?

Eve, falling into his snare, was deceived and ate of the forbidden fruit. Then she gave it to Adam, who also ate (Genesis 3:6). Thus, sin entered the human race.

While Satan used deception with Eve, he is not the reason sin entered the human race. Adam and Eve became sinners because they chose to disobey God. They sinned willfully. Satan didn't wrestle Adam to the ground and force him to eat a morsel of the forbidden fruit. Adam took a bite of the fruit willingly.

Transmission of Sin

What does Adam's sin have to do with the rest of us? After all, Adam lived thousands of years ago. The answer is that we sinned in Adam.

7. Read Romans 5:12. What chance does a person have of being born sinless according to this verse?

The proof that we all have sinned in Adam is that death, the penalty for sin, has passed on to Adam's descendants. Both the physical and the spiritual parts of a person are derived from the parents, originating at conception. Therefore, man is born with a sin nature, which goes back to Adam.

Someone might ask, "Is it fair that all humans should suffer from the sin of one man?" Divine justice answers yes, because the suffering of one man—Jesus Christ—can save all humankind. This is the point of Romans 5:12–21. While all people are lost because of Adam's sin, all can be saved because of Jesus Christ's obedience.

8. When do parents usually begin to see evidence that their children were born sinners?

Practice of Sin

Man is a sinner by nature and by act.

9. How would you define sin?

Sin is generally an infraction of any of God's commands; it is anything that does not conform to the holiness of God. Isaiah used several different words for sin in Isaiah 53. Verses 5 and 8 call a person's failure "transgression." Verse 12 uses another form of the word, translated "transgressors." This word, used about 90 times in the Old Testament, is usually translated "transgression." It is sometimes synonymous with sin, but at times it suggests a violation of law through ignorance.

In verses 6, 8, and 11, Isaiah used "iniquity," which carries the idea of perversity or depravity. The word "sin" (v. 12) contains the thought of missing the mark or swerving aside. In the New Testament, sin is defined as lawlessness (1 John 3:4), that is, a violation of God's law. After quoting a number of Old Testament passages to prove the point, Paul clearly stated, "all have sinned" (Romans 3:23).

Isaiah certainly believed that all men are sinners. He wrote, "All we like sheep have gone astray; we have turned every one to his own way" (Isaiah 53:6). These words vividly picture the sinfulness of all humanity; we have all missed the mark and are headed in the wrong direction. Instead of pursuing God's will, we are all seeking our own way.

10. Read Isaiah 53:6. Why is a wandering sheep a good illustration of a sinner?

Penalty for Sin

But is sin serious? Since everyone sins, can't we just accept it and live with it? The fact is, we cannot live with it, for sin "bringeth forth death" (James 1:15). Because sin violates God's law, a punishment must be paid. God told Adam not to eat of the forbidden tree, explaining, "For in the day that thou eatest thereof thou shalt surely die" (Genesis 2:17). The apostle Paul wrote that "the wages of sin is death" (Romans 6:23), and we find the death penalty for sin repeated in Ezekiel 18:4.

11. Read Ezekiel 18:4. What is the plain truth stated in this verse?

Hence, since all people are sinners, then all are under the sentence of death. The sentence of death must be met. Divine justice requires payment. We cannot ignore sin. No one can pay the penalty him- or herself.

12. Read Revelation 20:10–15. Why is paying for one's sin impossible?

Someone else must pay the penalty for the sinner. Every person needs the only suitable substitute, Jesus Christ. He paid the full price for our sins.

Submissive Attitude

Having established that man needs a substitute, we have a problem: where can we find a suitable one. In previous studies, we found that Christ is indeed a suitable substitute. But the question remains whether He was willing to be our substitute.

We find embodied in the language of Isaiah 53 proof that Messiah submitted Himself to the suffering He endured.

13. What do we learn about Christ from the passive verbs used about His suffering in Isaiah 53? For example, in verse 5 it says Christ *was wounded* for our transgressions.

The language that talks about the suffering of Christ in Isaiah 53 is in the passive voice, which means that Christ did not take the action. Christ was acted upon. He "was wounded," not that He "wounded himself." He "was oppressed," "was afflicted," "[was] taken from prison," "[was] cut off," "[was] stricken," and "[was] numbered." Christ allowed the suffering to be brought on Himself. He did not resist it or turn from it.

Note also that "the Lord hath laid on him the iniquity of us all" (v. 6) and that "it pleased the Lord to bruise him, he hath put him to grief" (v. 10). Both God and man had a part in the Lord's suffering. Yet Christ submitted to it. "He shall see of the travail of his soul, and shall be satisfied; . . . for he shall bear their iniquities" (v. 11). And in verse 12, we read that "he bore the sin of many."

Opened Not His Mouth

Verse 7 is the clearest statement of His voluntary submission: "He was oppressed, and he was afflicted, yet he opened not his mouth: he is brought as a lamb to the slaughter, and as a sheep before her shearers is dumb, so he openeth not his mouth." Unlike the wayward sheep in verse 6, Christ was the quiet, submissive sheep Who became the sacrificial Lamb of God (John 1:29).

Christ is pictured in the New Testament as the Good Shepherd who willingly gave His life for His sheep.

One might ask when Jesus Christ's submissive spirit began. Luke recorded an interesting account when, as a boy of twelve, Jesus accompanied the family on the yearly visit to Jerusalem to celebrate the Passover (Luke 2:41). While Jesus was in Jerusalem, His well-known encounter with the teachers at the temple occurred. After that He "went down with them [his parents], and came to Nazareth, and was subject unto them" (Luke 2:51). Jesus, "increased in wisdom . . . and in favour with God and man" (v. 52). He was never smart mouthed or rebellious. Before He began His public ministry, He was submissive to the authority of his earthly parents.

He was also submissive to His Heavenly Father. In Gethsemane He prayed, "Nevertheless not my will, but thine, be done" (Luke 22:42) just before the Crucifixion. His prayer showed His continuing submission to

God the Father. He also testified, “I can of mine own self do nothing: as I hear, I judge: and my judgment is just; because I seek not mine own will, but the will of the Father which hath sent me” (John 5:30).

In 1 Peter 2:21 Peter addressed slaves who received harsh treatment from their masters. He encouraged them to take such treatment patiently. He explained, “For even hereunto were ye called: because Christ also suffered for us, leaving us an example, that ye should follow his steps.” Christ’s suffering provides not only our salvation, but also a proper way to view mistreatment.

Substitutionary Work

The Messiah endured suffering for us.

As an explanation of Jesus’ healing ministry, Matthew wrote, “That it might be fulfilled which was spoken by Esaias [Isaiah] the prophet, saying Himself took our infirmities, and bare our sicknesses” (Matthew 8:17).

14. Read Matthew 8:17. Have you ever heard of or talked to someone who believes that Jesus died on the cross to save us from our sicknesses in this life?

15. What do they conclude about those suffering from ailments and diseases?

Since Isaiah wrote in Hebrew, Matthew wrote in Greek and the text before us is in English, the wording is not identical, but clearly Matthew 8:17 is referring to the passage from Isaiah 53:4: “Surely he hath borne our griefs, and carried our sorrows.”

What is the explanation of the Matthew 8:17 passage? Matthew applied the passage to the work of Christ during His earthly ministry. This aspect of the prophecy was fulfilled sometime before the Cross. In addition, the miraculous healings the Lord performed were a preview of what He will do when He establishes His millennial Kingdom. Jesus announced His kingdom at the beginning of His ministry (Matthew 4:17). He attracted followers, preached about the kingdom, and healed all kinds of sickness to demonstrate what He could do and what it would be like in the messianic Kingdom.

Making It Personal

16. How should we respond to Jesus' willingness to suffer on the cross?

17. In what ministries are you only halfheartedly involved?

Remember Jesus' willingness to die for you when you are less than willing to serve Him.

18. Memorize Isaiah 53:6.

Lesson 10

The Triumphant Suffering of Messiah

Messiah's suffering produced many glorious results.

Isaiah 52:13—53:12

"He shall see of the travail of his soul, and shall be satisfied: by his knowledge shall my righteous servant justify many; for he shall bear their iniquities" (Isaiah 53:11).

Many mothers list childbirth as the most painful experience they have ever, and probably will ever, go through. So, why would a mother want to go through the pain two, three, or more times over? Why don't they stop having children? Because the joy on the other side of the pain is far greater than the pain.

The pain that Jesus experienced at the Cross was far greater than even the worst childbirth experience. But Christ doesn't regret the experience. The joy on the other side of the Cross outshines the pain.

Getting Started

1. What experience do you have with the pain and joy of childbirth?

2. What are other examples of pain followed by pleasure?

3. What gratification could Jesus have gotten from all the abuse heaped on Him?

Searching the Scriptures

This is the third study on Isaiah 53. The first one emphasized how the Messiah suffered; the second study looked at why He suffered. This study focuses on the results of His suffering.

Sepulcher for the Sacrifice

Christ's final words, "It is finished" (John 19:30), showed that He knew that His suffering was over, that He had paid the price, and that the redemptive process was completed. But what did God plan to do with His body?

Isaiah wrote, "He made his grave with the wicked" (Isaiah 53:9). A literal translation of this verse is, "One appointed his grave with the wicked." Those who crucified Him intended to do with His body what they did with the bodies of the two thieves they crucified with Him: bury them together (cf. John 19:31). However, God's divine plan preempted this human plan.

Isaiah continued, "and with the rich in his death" (Isaiah 53:9). As soon as Jesus' death was evident, Joseph of Arimathaea, a previously secret disciple and a rich man, "went to Pilate, and begged the body of Jesus . . . and laid it in his own new tomb" (Matthew 27:57–60; John 19:38–42), thus fulfilling Isaiah's prophecy.

Jesus' exaltation truly began with His burial. Joseph gave Him an honorable burial. Isaiah tells why the honorable burial was appropriate (Isaiah 53:9).

4. Read Isaiah 53:9. Why was an honorable burial for Jesus appropriate?

Father's Satisfaction

Another result of Christ's suffering was the Father's satisfaction. Messiah's suffering and its accomplishments pleased God the Father.

5. Read Isaiah 53:10 and Ezekiel 33:11. What apparent conflict arises when these verses are read together?

How could God take no pleasure in the death of the wicked yet be pleased by the death of His spotless Son? The answer is to look at God's pleasure from an eternal perspective. When the wicked die, they go to Hell. God doesn't delight in sending people to eternal torment (2 Peter 3:9), even though every human justly deserves it. When Christ died for the wicked, He provided every person a way to escape Hell and to enter Heaven. Christ's work pleased God because it was a perfect expression of His love for people.

Although Messiah's suffering culminated in His death, Isaiah 53:10 states, "He shall prolong his days." How can the days of someone who will die be prolonged? Christ's days were prolonged by His resurrection. Isaiah anticipated that the Messiah would not only die but that He would also rise again. In the first sermon preached after the Crucifixion, Peter presented the resurrection of Jesus as a proof that He was indeed the Messiah (Acts 2:25–31). Peter quoted from a psalm of David and pointed to David's tomb to prove that David had not been referring to his own resurrection but to Messiah's. Christ Himself taught about His resurrection, and all four of the Gospel writers recorded His words on the subject.

6. Read 1 Corinthians 15:17–23. Why is Christ's resurrection just as important as His substitutionary death?

Joy from Labor

7. When has your hard labor brought you joy?

Isaiah 53:11 speaks of Messiah's satisfaction. "Travail" refers to the labor pains a woman endures while giving birth. As a woman in labor gives birth to a child, so the pain Christ suffered gave birth to many children. In verse 10, Isaiah spoke of "his seed," meaning those who would become children of God through the new birth.

Isaiah 53:10 records another reference to God's satisfaction with Messiah's suffering: "And the pleasure of the Lord shall prosper in his hand." God was pleased with Christ because He did the Father's will.

8. Do you think that Jesus looked forward to pleasing the Father as a human son looks forward to pleasing his earthly father? Did Jesus care about what the Father thought of His work on the cross? Explain.

Different Perspective

Isaiah 53 was written from the perspective of Jews who were looking back at Jesus Christ's life and death, after they had come to realize that He is their Messiah. They expressed their doubts and misunderstandings of His suffering (53:1–4). Obviously, they were shocked to see how wrong they had been at the moment of His suffering. But those Jews aren't the only ones who will be surprised and amazed. Isaiah wrote, "As many were astonied [astonished or appalled] at thee" (52:14). People were amazed to learn that one who was exalted so high (v. 13) could have suffered so horribly. Even "the kings shall shut their mouths at him: for that which had not been told them shall they see; and that which they had not heard shall they consider" (v. 15). His exaltation gives them a totally different perspective.

Someday the sovereigns of this world will witness that "the kingdoms of this world are become the kingdoms of our Lord, and of his Christ; and he shall reign for ever and ever" (Revelation 11:15). Isaiah 52:13 states that Christ will "deal prudently," or wisely. The amazement of the world's sovereigns will aptly testify to His wise rule.

9. What usually happens to a politician's popularity once he or she takes office?

Jesus' rule will not have a drop in popularity. All will fully recognize Him as a wise and benevolent King.

Sprinkling

"So shall he sprinkle many nations" (Isaiah 52:15). Under the Levitical system, the priests of Israel used sprinkling to cleanse themselves (Leviticus 4:6; 8:17). "Sprinkling" can also refer to the spiritual cleansing of Gentiles who put their trust in Jesus Christ. ("Nations" can also speak of individual Gentiles, as it does here). From the beginning, this magnificent passage makes it evident that Messiah will have a ministry that is not limited to the Jewish people but that extends to the Gentiles as well.

Salvation Promise

Several phrases in chapter 53 speak directly of the salvation the Lord provided. "With his stripes we are healed" (v. 5) is quoted by Peter and applied to the salvation of the soul (1 Peter 2:24, 25). Clearly, Peter's use of the verse identifies Christ as both the sacrifice and the shepherd who provides salvation for those who turn to Him.

As noted earlier, Isaiah described Christ's suffering as travail (Isaiah 53:11) because it would produce born-again children. Paul used the same analogy to describe his own evangelistic work: "My little children, of whom I travail in birth again until Christ be formed in you" (Galatians 4:19; cf. 1 Thessalonians 2:9). Typically, for a child to be born, the mother must first experience labor, or travail. Likewise, for a person to be born again, someone somewhere has to travail for that person's soul.

10. How can we anguish, or travail (toil, labor, struggle, strain, work), for the souls of unsaved people?

Finally, consider the following phrase: "By his knowledge shall my righteous servant justify many" (Isaiah 53:11). "His knowledge" could refer to knowledge that Messiah possessed. The phrase could also refer to the knowledge of Jesus Christ that is necessary for justification. This view seems better than the first one. Certainly man needs a knowledge of Christ and of His redemptive work to be saved. This is the underlying idea in Romans 10.

11. Read Romans 10:13–15. What part do believers play in spreading the gospel message?

God provided salvation for all people, both Jew and Gentile. However, they have to know about this salvation before they can accept the offer. God has designed that people should hear the gospel from others who have already accepted Christ.

Supplication for the Sinner

Another element of Christ's victorious suffering relates to His resurrection: He intercedes for us. Isaiah 53 ends with the words, "He . . . made intercession for the transgressors" (v. 12). Who are the transgressors? They are the ones whose transgressions were laid on Him (v. 5). His intercession involves prayers for both those who rejected Him and those who receive Him.

12. Read Romans 8:33 and 34. How does knowing that Jesus prays directly to the Father for you affect your confidence in life?

On the cross Christ prayed, "Father, forgive them; for they know not what they do" (Luke 23:34). We assume the Lord Jesus was referring to the soldiers who had nailed Him to the cross. But because God laid "the iniquity of us all" on Him (53:6) we, too, are responsible for crucifying the Lord Jesus.

As you recall, Isaiah 53 was written from the view of Jews who assessed their mistaken thoughts during the Crucifixion. For those men, Jesus' prayer was answered; they were forgiven.

Conquering King

That terrible Crucifixion day must have looked like a horrible defeat for Jesus Christ, an ignominious end for one who had done so much good. But it was not the end. Resurrection morning came. He arose and later ascended to Heaven, where He is now at the right hand of God. One day, He will return to earth. When He does, the scenario will be entirely different.

Isaiah pictured Messiah as the conquering King who will divide the spoils with His followers: "Therefore will I divide him a portion with the great, and he shall divide the spoil with the strong" (53:12). The Jews of Isaiah's day understood the idea of a conquering king who claimed the spoils of war and shared them with his men. The kings of Israel had done that very thing (Genesis 14:16–24; 1 Samuel 30:20–26), and the Assyrian kings were doing that to Israel at the time.

Likewise, believers will receive a portion of the inheritance in

Christ's kingdom (Colossians 1:12, 13). We are heirs of God and joint-heirs with Christ (Romans 8:17); we will also reign with Him in His millennial Kingdom (cf. Revelation 2:26, 27; 3:21; 20:4, 6).

13. Read Isaiah 52:13. How might Christ be exalted and extolled, or lifted up, when He returns to earth at His Second Coming?

Earlier, Isaiah had seen the Lord "high and lifted up" (6:1). These two words are translated "exalted and extolled" in Isaiah 52:13. This is a regal position, as in Philippians 2:9–11. John envisioned Him as the "KING OF KINGS, AND LORD OF LORDS" (Revelation 19:16) who received "the kingdoms of this world" (Revelation 11:15) as He began His glorious reign.

A crown will follow the cross. Imagine the chagrin of Christ's enemies, of those who rejected Him and belittled His followers. Someday they will acknowledge that He is Lord.

14. Who are some notorious people who will seem out of place acknowledging Jesus as Lord?

Studying what God has in store for the future should be more than an intellectual pursuit for Christians. It should motivate us to godly living and instill in us a burning desire to warn the unsaved of their fate. Consider the words of 2 Peter 3:11: "Seeing then that all these things shall be dissolved, what manner of persons ought ye to be in all holy conversation and godliness?"

Making It Personal

15. What is it about the gospel message that makes us so afraid to share it?

16. Why aren't we more excited about sharing it?

Sharing the gospel is simply the common sense thing to do. The more you share it, the more natural it will become to you.

17. Memorize Isaiah 53:11.

Lesson 11

Messiah's Kingdom, Part 1

When Messiah establishes His kingdom, great physical changes will occur.

Selected verses

"The wilderness and solitary place shall be glad for them; and the desert shall rejoice, and blossom as the rose" (Isaiah 35:1).

When we speak of nature as being God's creation, we might cause a farmer to wrinkle his brow. Pests, weeds, and depleted soil are not exactly evidence that a perfect God created the earth. And the farmer would be right. The earth isn't the same as it was when God created it. Sin has brought a curse on creation. But when the Messiah returns He will cause changes in the ground, in the climate, and even in the animal life. The world will be closer to what it was like before the Fall.

Getting Started

1. What circumstances prevent someone from raising perfect crops or flowers?

2. Will it ever be possible to raise perfect crops? Explain

Searching the Scriptures

Isaiah is one of the richest books of the Bible regarding the messianic Kingdom. From beginning to end, it contains a multitude of references to the Kingdom.

Two interchangeable words describe Christ's coming kingdom: the messianic Kingdom and the millennial Kingdom. The word "messianic" reflects that the Messiah will rule this kingdom.

The word "millennial" refers to the duration of the Kingdom. The word "millennium" comes from the Latin word "mil" and literally means "one thousand years," the time Christ will reign on earth (Revelation 20:2–7).

This study takes a premillennial position, the view Baptists have historically held. However, there are other theological interpretations. At issue is when Christ's return will occur in relation to the Millennium and whether the Millennium is a literal earthly reign or a spiritual reign.

Premillennialism

This view teaches that Christ will return to earth before the Millennium. Seven years after the Rapture, He will return to earth with the elect to establish an earthly kingdom. He will rule from Jerusalem, fulfilling the promises and covenants made with Israel. He will judge the wicked, and only the righteous will enter His kingdom. Those who enter the Kingdom will still have physical bodies, and life will continue much as before, but the quality of life will be the highest it has been since the fall of man.

Postmillennialism

This position maintains that the gospel will overcome all evil and that the world will gradually get better until finally the golden age comes. Believers are to live godly lives, win others to Christ until the whole world is converted, and eventually bring in the Kingdom. Christ will return to earth after this age of peace (thus the use of the word "post"), judge the dead, and initiate the eternal state. World conditions of the past century have largely disproved this view, although it is experiencing resurgence.

3. What current world events would seem to prove that the world is actually getting worse rather than better?

Amillennialism

Amillennialists maintain that there is no Millennium. Strictly speaking, they believe in a Millennium but not a literal one. They believe that Christ's reign is occurring right now in believers' hearts. Essentially this view denies both the distinction between Israel and the Church and the literal interpretation of prophecy. It spiritualizes the prophecies concerning Israel's future, and applies them to the Church. When Christ does return to earth, amillennialists believe it will be to establish the eternal state. Ironically, this position holds that Satan is presently bound. A large segment of Christianity holds this view.

4. Why is spiritualizing Scripture a dangerous practice?

Premillennialism Defended

The strongest defense of this position is its basis on literal interpretation of Scripture. The Bible interpreter should interpret Scripture in the manner intended by God.

God made three great covenants that are foundational to the prophecies found in Isaiah. The covenants are in plain words and therefore demand a literal interpretation.

The **Abrahamic covenant** contains three elements: the promise of a seed (the nation Israel, the Jewish people); the promise of a land (Israel—from the borders of Egypt to the river Euphrates); and a blessing to all people (Christ). See Genesis 12:1–3; 13:14–17; and 17:2–6. This covenant is foundational to Isaiah 10:21, 22; 19:25; 43:1; and 65:8, 9.

5. Read Genesis 12:1–3. What, if anything, is complicated or mysterious about God's covenant to Abraham?

God promised in the **Davidic covenant** that one of David's seed, or descendants, would occupy Israel's throne forever (2 Samuel 7:12). That promise is behind Isaiah 11:1, 2 and 55:3, 11. The **Palestinian covenant**, which guarantees the land to Israel (Deuteronomy 30:1–10), is the basis of Isaiah 11:11, 12 and 65:9.

God gave Abrahamic, Davidic, and Palestinian covenants unconditionally; therefore, they are binding. God has never rescinded them, and He will see to it that they happen so that His word finds fulfillment. God will always fulfill His Word in the terms that He gave it.

6. What would life be like if we couldn't count on God to fulfill His word in the terms He gave it?

7. Which parts of the Abrahamic, Davidic, Palestinian, and New covenants has God not yet fulfilled?

God intends to keep His promises to Israel literally. For this reason, the premillennial position makes a distinction between Israel and the Church and reserves for Israel God's clear promises to the nation.

Regathering of Israel

During the Millennium, Israel will again be at the center of God's program. The Jews will occupy the land promised to the seed of Abraham.

The Jewish people are scattered throughout the world. Today's world population of Jews is about 14 million. One day they will all return to Israel, the land promised to Abraham (Genesis 15:18–21).

8. Read Genesis 15:18–21. Has Israel ever yet possessed all this land?

God will gather Israel, an object of His love.

9. Read Isaiah 43:5–7. What language in this passage helps to communicate the special place Israel will have in God's heart in the Millennium?

Restored Kingdom

After the regathering of Israel, Messiah will reign on the throne of David (Isaiah 9:6, 7). His rule will be severe (Isaiah 11:4; cf. Psalm 2:8–12), but it will be righteous too (Isaiah 32:1). God will fulfill His promise to David that one of his offspring would sit on the throne (2 Samuel 7:12). Israel's greatness will exceed anything she has known before (Isaiah 60). Israel will be in a position of honor; other nations will enjoy God's blessings as well (cf. 19:24, 25).

Not only will Israel be in the center of God's spotlight, but Jerusalem will be the center of world interest and worship.

10. Read Isaiah 2:2 and 3. What does this passage say about the place of Jerusalem in the Millennium?

Ezekiel extensively described the millennial temple in Jerusalem and the worship that will take place there (Ezekiel 40—46). Jerusalem will be a glorious city (Isaiah 52:1–12; 60:14–21; 61:3), and God will protect it and the nation (Isaiah 33:20–24).

Waste Places Reconstructed

During the Tribulation, many battles will take place in Israel, and the land will be devastated. But God will reclaim the land and make it ready for habitation.

Ravaged, desolate places will be built up and fully occupied (49:19; 61:4; cf. 32:16–18).

At times in Israel's history, because of the nation's sin, the people saw their cities captured and inhabited by invaders. However, during the Millennium, things will be different.

11. Read Isaiah 65:21 and 22. What does this passage say about the reconstruction of Israel?

Also, during the Millennium, a new population explosion will occur, because there will be peace, prosperity, and plenty of food (26:15; 49:19; 29:16). People will live to be much older than they are now (65:20). Conditions will be ideal for an increase in population, and the world will be able to sustain it.

Desert Rejuvenation

Israel has not always been as it is today. The area around the Dead Sea today is quite desolate. It is amazing to think that Lot once chose those areas because they were "well watered every where . . . as the garden of the Lord" (Genesis 13:10). This garden-like plain was once the site of several large cities. But God warned His people that if they disobeyed Him, He would discipline them by withholding the rain, a fact very evident today. Nevertheless, the potential for productivity still exists, locked away beneath the soil.

One day, the rains will return (Isaiah 30:23). "In the wilderness shall waters break out, and streams in the desert. And the parched ground shall become a pool, and the thirsty land springs of water: in the habitation of dragons [jackals], where each lay, shall be grass and reeds and rushes" (35:6, 7; cf. 41:17, 18; 49:10).

The increased rainfall will cause an agricultural boom. Many references speak of the bounty of harvest during Messiah's kingdom (35:1, 2; 32:15; 29:17; 51:3). Every harvest will yield a bumper crop (65:23). God told Adam that he'd have to labor and struggle with weeds to produce his crops (Genesis 3:18). But during the Millennium, there will be no weed-control problems (55:13).

12. Read Amos 9:13. What did Amos prophecy about the Millennium?

This potential is evident today. Wherever water is available for irrigation, the desert has already "blossomed as the rose" and has produced much food. However, current agricultural increase is nothing compared to what the land will see when Christ comes to rule.

Restructured Animals

When Adam sinned, the curse fell on man, on the earth, and on the animals. God cursed the serpent, who was an instrument of Satan and the representative of the animal kingdom (Genesis 3:14, 15), and the other animals suffered under that curse.

In the original creation, man and beast were both herbivorous (Genesis 1:29, 30). As a result of the Fall, certain animals became carnivorous and ferocious. After the Flood, man, too, became a meat eater (Genesis 9:2, 3).

13. Read Isaiah 11:6–8. What do you find most intriguing about the change in wildlife during the Millennium?

During the Millennium, Edenic conditions will return. Peace will exist within the animal kingdom. No longer will animals have a predator-prey relationship. Cows and bears, leopards and kids, and wolves and lambs will live together in harmony, unafraid of one another. Ferocious animals will no longer threaten man (11:6). "The sucking child shall play on the hole of the asp, and the weaned child shall put his hand on the cockatrice' den" (11:8). The asp and the cockatrice are deadly poisonous snakes, but during the Millennium, they will pose no threat to man.

However, it is significant that the serpent will continue in its state of the curse: "And dust shall be the serpent's meat" (Isaiah 65:25; cf. Genesis 3:14). Many believe that the serpent originally walked but was condemned to crawl because of its part in the fall of man and that it will never regain its original status.

During the messianic Kingdom, all creation will be restored to conditions similar to those before the Fall (Rom. 8:19–21). The redemption of nature is coupled with the final redemption (glorification) of the believer.

These future changes will occur because of the sacrificial work of Jesus Christ on the cross. Other changes will also occur when Christ institutes the eternal state (cf. Revelation 21:1). At the conclusion of the Millennium, the curse will be completely removed (Revelation 22:3). God will continue to reign throughout the eternal state. In the meantime, believers should diligently study the Scripture, holding firmly to the truths it teaches (Revelation 1:3). We must realize that the Word of God, which assures us of our salvation, also assures us of God's future work, which is a part of our salvation.

Making It Personal

14. Which Bible character are you looking forward to spending time with in the Millennium the most?

15. What do you think you will talk about?

16. Only those who receive Christ as their Savior will enter Christ's Millennial Kingdom. Who do you know that is currently not on the list of invited guests? What can you do to invite him or her today?

17. Memorize Isaiah 35:1.

Lesson 12

Messiah's Kingdom, Part 2

Righteousness will characterize Messiah's Kingdom.

Selected verses

"And many people shall go and say, Come ye, and let us go up to the mountain of the LORD, to the house of the God of Jacob; and he will teach us of his ways, and we will walk in his paths: for out of Zion shall go forth the law, and the word of the LORD from Jerusalem" (Isaiah 2:3).

War protestors have a simplistic view of the world. They believe that everyone should stop fighting and just get along. That sounds like an easy solution. But it would never work. Why? Because the world has hateful, sinful men who would take over every country or land they could until someone challenged them. The challenge would most likely start a new war.

When Christ comes back to set up his Kingdom, war will be no more. That is hard to imagine.

Getting Started

1. Will there ever be peace in Israel?

2. Can humans bring peace to the world?

Searching the Scripture

The last lesson described physical changes that will occur to the land during the messianic Kingdom. This lesson will emphasize the spiritual dimension of the Kingdom.

Return of the Messiah

The Old Testament didn't distinguish between the first and second comings of Christ. While the prophets wrote about both events, they did not realize that an extended time would elapse between the Lord's first earthly ministry (which ended in His death) and His future earthly ministry (which will begin with the establishment of His kingdom). The Old Testament prophets wrote about Christ's suffering and His glory, but they could not reconcile those twin truths in their minds. Isaiah, like all the other prophets, intertwined the two truths without clearly distinguishing between them.

3. Read Isaiah 52:13–15. Which parts of this passage are referring to Christ's first coming and which are referring to His second?

From other passages, we can learn that the messianic Kingdom will begin when Christ returns to earth after the Tribulation (Revelation 19:11–21). Isaiah did not write about the Second Coming, but he did prophesy much about the Lord's reign after His return. Consider some of the events that will accompany the establishment of the Kingdom.

The Reckoning of the Living

Only believers will enter the millennial Kingdom. Daniel predicted that "the saints of the most High shall take the kingdom, and possess the kingdom for ever, even for ever and ever" (Daniel 7:18). This verse means that God must judge and destroy the unsaved before the Kingdom begins. Isaiah predicted that the Messiah would proclaim "the day of vengeance of our God" (Isaiah 61:2b). Previously, we learned that Jesus read Isaiah 61:1 and 2a when He preached at Nazareth. He told the people that Scripture was then being fulfilled. Notice He did not include the last part of the verse, the portion that speaks of the "day of vengeance." Why? Simply because that part would not be fulfilled at His first coming; vengeance or judgment will occur at His second coming. There will be separate judgments for the Jews and the Gentiles.

Ezekiel 20:33–38 predicted a judgment of Israel in the wilderness, in which Christ will purge the rebels. Isaiah did not give details of this judgment but assumed a judgment that leaves only the repentant to enter the Kingdom. Not only will Messiah proclaim "the day of vengeance of our God," but He will also "comfort all that mourn" (61:2b, 3). Righteousness is a key word; it describes the spiritual condition that will prevail during the Millennium.

Isaiah 34 is a prophecy of the judgment of Gentiles.

4. Read Isaiah 34:1, 2. How do these verses describe the judgment on the Gentiles?

Joel 3:1–17 and Matthew 25:31–46 further describe this judgment, a judgment based on the Gentiles' treatment of Israel. Matthew wrote that God will usher these righteous (sheep) Gentiles into the Kingdom (cf. Isaiah 56:1–8). Isaiah wrote that Egypt and Assyria will have a place in Messiah's Kingdom (19:24, 25), and Zechariah specifically mentioned Egypt as worshiping in Jerusalem (Zechariah 14:18, 19).

5. Read Isaiah 63:1–6. How is Christ's judgment of the Gentiles pictured in this passage?

6. Why is trampling grapes a good illustration of God's wrath?

Revelation 19:11–21 presents this judgment as a victorious warrior leading his troops against the armies of the world. Isaiah 12—23 predicts the judgment of many of the Gentile nations around Israel.

The Regeneration of Israel

In these judgments, God will judge the unrighteous, but will allow the saved to enter the Kingdom. Salvation will come to those who look to God: "Look unto me, and be ye saved, all the ends of the earth: for I am God, and there is none else" (45:22).

Isaiah 44:22–24 records the beautiful promise of forgiveness given to Israel.

7. Isaiah 44:22–24. What pictures does God use to demonstrate His forgiveness of Israel?

8. What is the mood in this passage?

In Isaiah 35:10, the prophet wrote concerning the "ransomed" who will inhabit the Kingdom. Israel will also be called "the redeemed of the Lord" (62:12). Isaiah's use of the terms "ransomed" and "redeemed" refers to the price Jesus Christ paid on the cross, when He bore "the iniquity of us all" (53:6). Israel will someday recognize that Jesus is indeed the Messiah, their "offering for sin" (53:10). This redemption is a work of God (43:1; 45:25; 59:20).

Political Conditions

The nature of the government of Messiah's Kingdom is embodied within its name; the Messiah will rule. Isaiah wrote, "The government shall be upon his [Christ's] shoulder" (9:6, 7).

The Lord Jesus Christ will be the head of the government during the Millennium, and He will administer His kingdom through an organizational structure. The Lord will apparently resurrect David and make him regent in the Kingdom (Isaiah 55:3, 4). Other resurrected saints will rule with Him (Matthew 19:28; Revelation 2:27; 3:21; 20:4, 6).

Messiah will have judges and princes who assist him (Isaiah 1:26; 32:1). Although Isaiah did not mention it, Christ will resurrect the Church saints and the Tribulation martyrs to reign with Him.

9. Think of the humblest, godliest foreign missionary you know. Now imagine him or her ruling over the same section of the world for the Lord during the Millennium. What thoughts come to your mind as you imagine such a scene?

During the Millennium, national distinctions will continue to exist. Israel will be the world's most favored nation. Because Messiah will rule as king, Israel will no longer live in fear of foreign invasion; the Lord will defend her (Isaiah 33:17–22).

According to Isaiah 14:1, God will also include Gentiles in the Kingdom, as servants of Israel (49:22, 23; 61:5). Egypt and Assyria will have a place in the Kingdom but will be subject to Israel (19:16–25; cf. 60:14–17).

The Strength of the Government

The strength of the millennial Kingdom will be in its leader, the Messiah. He will rule with a rod of iron (Psalm 2:9; Isaiah 11:3–5).

Because God will destroy the enemy and Christ will rule absolutely, universal peace will follow. Isaiah called the Messiah the "Prince of peace" (9:6). War will be no more (2:4; Micah 4:3).

Prosperity will be follow peace, which will sustain the government. Unrest and poverty contribute to the overthrow of governments, but since those conditions won't be present, Messiah's kingdom will be strong.

10. Read Isaiah 9:7. How is the strength of Christ's Kingdom described in this verse?

The everlasting promise given to God's people guarantees an everlasting kingdom (51:6–8; 55:13; 60:19, 20; 61:8).

Economic Conditions

Today many countries' economies face an uphill struggle. Government overspending, conflicting priorities among leaders, and labor struggles contribute to the problem. Human reasoning and social engineering have seemingly only made things worse. A change of political administration seldom results in long-range solutions. During the Millennium, when Jesus Christ reigns, the government will produce a perfectly healthy economy.

In times of repression, conquering nations often make subdued people provide food for them. For example, during the days of Gideon, the Midianites confiscated what Israel grew (Judges 6:1–6). Under Communist rule, Russia skimmed off the best from the nations it controlled. However, under Messiah's just rule, it will not be that way.

11. Read Isaiah 62:8 and 9. What makes the Lord's promise so sure?

Labor will not be in vain, and children will not be born into a life of poverty (65:21–23).

Messiah's righteous rule will affect even the physical environment. The land will be unusually productive, and the parched land of Israel will blossom like a rose (Isaiah 35:1, 2). The Lord will restore the rains that He had withheld because of the people's sin. The booming agricultural production will result in a vigorous economy (30:23–26). Today many parts of the world face starvation because of war, drought, or mismanagement. During the Millennium there will be no lack of food and, therefore, no starvation.

12. Have you experienced poverty at some point in your life? What was it like?

The cost of health care is a hot topic. Many people can't afford decent health care. The health care in many third-world countries is almost nonexistent. During the Millennium, however, people will live long, healthy lives. Christ will heal diseases (33:24; 29:17–19; 35:3–6); food will be plentiful; wars will not take their toll; the curse of sin will be gone. "There shall be no more thence an infant of days, nor an old man that hath not filled his days" (65:20). God will preserve life supernaturally (41:8–14; 62:8, 9).

Spiritual Conditions

Wickedness is the rule on the earth today. During the Millennium, however, righteousness and godliness will characterize the people.

During the Millennium, the Messiah's followers will reflect His characteristics. This likeness will be more than a mimicking of a popular figure; it will result from a spiritual change caused by God's work of redemption. The people of the Kingdom will be righteous (9:7, 60:21, 26:2) and holy.

Throughout the Millennium, people will worship God in Zion. Isaiah 2:3 states it beautifully: "And many people shall go and say, Come ye, and let us go up to the mountain of the Lord, to the house of the God of Jacob; and he will teach us of his ways, and we will walk in his paths: for out of Zion shall go forth the law, and the word of the Lord from Jerusalem." There also will be a unified worship (45:23; 27:13).

Prayer has always been an important part of the believer's life. Will it be necessary in the Millennium when the Lord is present to meet all our needs? Surprisingly, the believer will still pray, and he has a wonderful prayer promise to encourage him.

13. Read Isaiah 65:24. What is the promise for those who pray in the Millennium?

God has also given many prayer promises to the believer today. If people will pray during the Millennium, is there not an even greater need for believers to pray today?

Making It Personal

14. What excites you the most about the Millennium?

15. How should the fact of the Millennium affect your life today?

16. Memorize Isaiah 2:3.

Lesson 13

Messiah's Invitation to Salvation

God offers free salvation to all who will accept it.

Isaiah 55:1—56:2

"Seek the LORD while he may be found, call ye upon him while he is near: let the wicked forsake his way, and the unrighteous man his thoughts: and let him return unto the LORD, and he will have mercy upon him; and to our God, for he will abundantly pardon" (Isaiah 55:6, 7).

If a company is offering you something free, then put your hand on your wallet because the company probably wants your money. Even free samples that come in the mail are simply a way to entice you to buy the product in the store. They want you to like the product enough to want more of it. But getting more will cost you your money.

Getting Started

1. When have you had to spend money in order to get something for "free"?

2. Can you name one thing that is truly free?

Searching the Scriptures

Isaiah 55 is truly one of the most beautiful chapters of the Old Testament. Preachers have called it the John 3:16 of the Old Testament and the "gospel according to Isaiah." It records God's free offer of salvation to anyone who acknowledges his need.

Isaiah 55:1–3a applied to the captive Jews in Babylon. Isaiah encouraged them not to seek satisfaction in the vain material things in Babylon but to return to their homeland. Israel's deliverance from Babylon pictures the soul's redemption, made possible by Messiah's sacrificial work.

Universal Appeal

Isaiah 55 begins with "Ho," a somewhat cryptic word used to call attention to an important announcement. Through Isaiah God was about to make an offer of great significance; it was as welcome as water to thirsty desert travelers. He made the offer to the thirsty, the hungry, and the needy. While verse 1 may seem to limit the offer to the poor and needy, the context shows that, all people are needy because their money cannot buy satisfaction (v. 2).

3. How can we help people see their need of salvation?

Unusual Offer

God's offer included items every person needs (v. 1). He offered water, wine, and milk, some of life's necessities, and items that were easily recognizable as such in the simple Israelite culture. Water is life's most basic need, yet it was often scarce in the arid East. Christ is the living water who meets our most basic spiritual need.

Wine was a common drink in Bible times. It symbolized joy and happiness (Judges 9:13; Psalm 104:15). In Isaiah 55:1, the prophet used it to suggest the joy of salvation. Milk was another basic commodity in Palestine's agrarian economy and was a necessity of life. In Scripture, milk often represents nourishment (Exodus 3:8; 1 Peter 2:2). Isaiah's offer of milk suggests that the gospel will meet the fundamental needs of sinful man.

In our market-driven society, we often see products we really want and need but just can't afford. What about God's offer? It is for the person who "hath no money" (55:1) and is affordable to all. Salvation is a commodity marketed "without money and without price" (55:1).

Unprofitable Quest

Verse two describes man's fruitless and frustrating efforts to find satisfaction. This verse suggests that the water, wine, and milk of verse 1 symbolize spiritual realities. Thirst is a good analogy for the longing a person feels inside to be whole. All people have a spiritual thirst that only God can fill. Verse 2 points out this truth.

4. Read Isaiah 55:2. To what do people turn in their quest to satisfy the thirsting of their souls?

5. What was your life like before you came to Christ? How real was the thirsting of your souls?

Verse 2 asks, "Wherefore do ye spend money for that which is not bread?" The things that people can buy with their money won't meet their basic spiritual needs. They can't buy their salvation.

Many people love their jobs and find great fulfillment in a job well done. However, no one can find satisfaction by trying to work out his or her salvation. No one can ever know if he or she has done enough works or the right works, because salvation is "not of works" (Ephesians 2:9). When people try to work for their salvation, they bring themselves only frustration, dissatisfaction, and uncertainty.

Uncomplicated Requirement

The word "come" appears four times in Isaiah 55:1–3; the repetition of the word shows the importance of the invitation. "Hearken diligently" is the translation of a Hebrew construction that makes the statement even more imperative. It means, "hear carefully." The third verse picks up the command again: "hear, and your soul shall live."

Knowing the facts of salvation is not enough—one must act on that knowledge. In other words, a person must hear God's appeal, obey God's Word, and respond to His invitation.

6. Why does the simplicity of salvation sometimes keep people from accepting it?

Unending Result

Things we can buy or earn are worthless when compared to what God offers. He gives life to those who hear and heed His appeal. Isaiah put it this way: "Your soul shall live" (v. 3a). He presented the idea that God's salvation offers eternal life.

7. In what ways have you found satisfaction in your salvation?

8. Read Matthew 5:6. What connection can you see between this verse and what Isaiah wrote in 55:2: "Let your soul delight itself in fatness"?

The Covenant

Isaiah 55:3b–5 assures us that the blessings offered in the invitation are permanent. God promises to make a covenant with those who respond to the gracious invitation.

Isaiah referred to the Davidic Covenant: "I will make an everlasting covenant with you, even the sure mercies of David" (v. 3). This covenant rests on God's earlier promise that one of David's seed would occupy the throne of Israel forever (2 Samuel 7:14). Paul referred to "the sure mercies of David" in Acts 13:34, where he presented Christ as the fulfillment of the Old Testament prophecies and the justifier of all who believe on Him (13:32–39). This covenant is the guarantee that God will keep His word and give life to the recipient of His gracious offer.

9. Why is being assured that God will keep Word so important to the Christian life?

The witness, leader, and commander described in verse 4 ultimately refers to Jesus Christ. Although David was a witness for God, a leader and a commander of his people, he foreshadowed his Greater Son, the Messiah, who would fulfill the covenant God had made with David. Verse 5 confirms this conclusion, since Christ calls to nations who respond to Him.

Christ is indeed our leader and our commander, and He has had a good witness. Because He is a leader and commander, His subjects should follow and obey Him. To Israel, God said, "Ye are my witnesses" (Isaiah 43:10, 12; 44:8). Christ told His disciples, "Ye shall be witnesses" (Acts 1:8).

The nations of verse 5 are Gentiles nations that Messiah will invite to obtain the priceless blessings described in verse 1.

The Conversion

Isaiah 55:6 holds an important truth concerning salvation: "Seek ye the Lord while he may be found, call ye upon him while he is near." The Lord has not always been available, and He will not always be available. One must never presume that he or she will have opportunity to trust Christ later. Life is uncertain; death is sure. Therefore, people must seize the offer of salvation immediately. Few Gentiles had this opportunity in the Old Testament (Acts 17:30), but now during the Church Age the Lord offers salvation to all nations (Matthew 28:19, 20).

10. How are your witnessing efforts affected when you hear about a sudden death?

Isaiah 55:7 describes the person who has accepted the invitation in verse 1: "Let the wicked forsake his way, and the unrighteous man his thoughts: and let him return unto the Lord." The forsaking of sin is not a requirement for salvation; it is rather the expected result of salvation. A change in the believer's life should take place. Christians frequently quote Ephesians 2:8 and 9 to prove that salvation is by faith alone, but all too often we overlook verse ten: "For we are his workmanship, created in Christ Jesus unto good works, which God hath before ordained that we should walk in them." We aren't saved *by* good works but *to* good works. God expects the believer's new life to be different from his old life.

11. What was the biggest difference in your life right after you were saved?

The idea continues in verse 7: "He will have mercy upon him; and to our God, for he will abundantly pardon." God pardons, and He does so abundantly. Some people realize their great sin when they come to Christ; others may not recognize just how sinful they are until after they've been saved and studied God's Word. Regardless, there is abundant pardon for all.

The Comparison

God's thoughts and ways are different from man's. This truth is obvious, so why mention it here (Isaiah 55:8, 9)? Because God's work of salvation is something that man could not do nor could he even imagine it. In verse 8, God declared that His dealings with people are different from what people would have thought.

12. Isaiah 55:8 and 9. What are some ways of salvation that might seem more logical than God's way of salvation?

To help us understand how different God's ways are from ours, Isaiah pointed the reader to the skies: a vast expanse separates the heavens from the earth. A gap of even greater magnitude—one that is infinite—separates God and man.

Just as the rain helps the earth produce a harvest, so God's word will produce a result: "It shall not return unto me void, but it shall accomplish that which I please, and it shall prosper in the thing whereto I send it (Isaiah 55:10, 11). What God says is trustworthy and powerful. No one can claim that God is not able to keep His word.

Contentment

Isaiah 55 closes with an outburst of rejoicing. The salvation promised in this chapter is certainly cause for joy. Peace, one of the provisions of justification (Romans 5:1), is often connected to joy (Romans 15:13; Galatians 5:22).

13. When have you met a person and surmised that he or she was probably a believer just by the expression on his or her face?

Isaiah used some descriptive, figurative language to get his point across.

He pictured the mountains and hills singing and the trees clapping their hands. Paul wrote in Romans 8:22 that nature itself, being under the curse of sin, is groaning and waiting for the deliverance Christ will bring when He comes again.

As we saw in lesson 11, during the Millennium, the physical environment will undergo great change. Edenic conditions will return: animals will lose their wild nature (Isaiah 11:6–9), and the thorns and briars will give way to fir and myrtle trees (55:13). The curse will be lifted because of Christ's redemptive work.

The thought of God's salvation continues in chapter 56. God expects justice and righteousness from the believer. They are the outworking of salvation.

God will bless the person who lives a righteous life.

Making It Personal

14. What do people see expressed on your face as you go about your life?

15. What should they see on your face?

16. How should knowing the peace and joy of the Lord affect your witness?

Wear the hope of salvation on your face wherever you go.

17. Memorize Isaiah 55:6 and 7.